D1480435

SOUL OF GOODNESS

Transform Grievous Hurt, Betrayal, and Setback into Love, Joy, and Compassion

Christopher Phillips, PhD

Prometheus Books

Guilford, Connecticut

Prometheus Books

An imprint of The Rowman & Littlefield Publishing Group, Inc.
4501 Forbes Boulevard, Suite 200
Lanham, Maryland 20706
www.rowman.com

Distributed by NATIONAL BOOK NETWORK

British Library Cataloguing in Publication Information Available

Library of Congress Cataloging-in-Publication Data

Names: Phillips, Christopher, 1959 July 15– author.
Title: Soul of goodness : transform grievous hurt, betrayal, and setback into love, joy, and compassion / Christopher Phillips, PhD.
Description: Lanham, MD : Prometheus, [2022] | Summary: "This moving, insightful and ultimately hopeful and helpful blend of memoir and philosophical exploration begins in Christopher Phillips's native stomping grounds of the tiny volcanic island of Nisyros, Greece and unfurls through space and time as the author explores the connections between his immediate circumstances and the eternal wisdom of popular philosophers"— Provided by publisher.
Identifiers: LCCN 2021023896 (print) | LCCN 2021023897 (ebook) | ISBN 9781633887886 (cloth) | ISBN 9781633887893 (epub)
Subjects: LCSH: Soul. | Good and evil. | Conduct of life. | Phillips, Christopher, 1959 July 15–
Classification: LCC BD423 .P45 2022 (print) | LCC BD423 (ebook) | DDC 128/.1—dc23
LC record available at https://lccn.loc.gov/2021023896
LC ebook record available at https://lccn.loc.gov/2021023897

∞™ The paper used in this publication meets the minimum requirements of American National Standard for Information Sciences Permanence of Paper for Printed Library Materials, ANSI/NISO Z39.48-1992.

For my loves Cecilia, Cali, and Cybele

My beloved dad, Alexander Phillips

And my true-blue brothers,
Cornel West and Dennis Dienst

"There is some soul of goodness in things evil, would
men observingly distill it out.
For our bad neighbors make us early stirrers, which is
both healthful and good husbandry;
besides, they are our outward consciences, and preachers
to us all, admonishing that we should dress us fairly."
—William Shakespeare, Henry V, Act 4, Scene 1

"To suffer woes which Hope thinks infinite; to forgive
wrongs darker than death or night;
to defy Power, which seems omnipotent;
To love, and bear;
to hope till Hope creates from its own wreck
the thing it contemplates.
Neither to change nor falter nor repent; This . . . is to be
Good, great and joyous, beautiful and free."
—Percy Bysshe Shelley, Prometheus Unbound

CONTENTS

FOREWORD

Dr. Cornel West

Christopher Phillips is the greatest living embodiment of the Socratic spirit in our catastrophic times. His global grassroots movement of Socrates Cafés and Democracy Cafés have transformed the lives of millions of people in every continent on the earth. His brilliant and wise books have touched the minds and souls of so many of us. And his soulful style and genuine compassion have enriched the lives of us fortunate ones. When the historians write of the ugly and beautiful in our turbulent age, the Socratic words, works, and deeds of my dearest Brother Christopher Phillips should loom large.

Yet how did Philip Christoforos Philipou come to be the humble and towering figure so loved and respected around the world? This powerful personal and profound philosophical book is a painful though joyful historical self-inventory of the makings of his exemplary life. This candid text lays bare the raw realities and refined visions of his courageous quest for Plato's "healthy soul" and Shakespeare's "soul of goodness." Like the great Percy Shelley's recasting of Aeschylus in *Prometheus Bound*, Christopher Phillips takes us on his own philosopher's path to "be good, great, joyous, beautiful and free."

Christopher Phillips's beloved grandmother, Calliope Kavazarakis Philipou—his *yaya* and close reader of great Greek texts—gives
him a birthday gift of Plato's Socratic dialogues and lovingly says,
"You are the one who will be like his protagonist, Socrates." This
prophetic pronouncement rings true like the Delphic Oracle of
"Know thyself" to Socrates. From the village of Mandraki on the
island of Nisyros on the Aegean Sea to the towns of Newport
News, Virginia, and Tampa, Florida, Christopher's pilgrimage will
crystallize into a tear-soaked and bloodstained struggle to carry
"the Socratic torch." The mysterious death of his beloved father
and the magnanimous love of his magnificent wife sit at the dynamic center of this spirit-filled and quest-driven struggle. For Phillips, the examined life is worth dying for and the committed life
yields ineffable joys. To put it bluntly, the joyful and majestic
dance of Christopher and Ceci (his heaven-sent wife) to Afro-Cuban Ray Barreto's "Acid" moved me to tears.

Like Chaucer's Pilgrim and Dante's Sojourner, Phillips embod-
ies and exemplifies the funk of loss and betrayal, hurt and grief,
alongside joy and compassion. Like Hermes, Phillips helps us to
learn how to see, feel, and act more humanly and humanely through
his many travels around the world. His heartfelt experience with
fragile Melinda and forceful Keshia cut deep. His multicultural
explorations into *batsil winic* (true human), *ningen* (in-between
persons), and *ubuntu* (I am in you and you are in me) of the life-
worlds of indigenous peoples, Japanese peoples, and African peoples reveal the Socratic spirit at its best. One of my favorite moments is his engagement with *saudade* (irremediable grief and irre-
pressible joy). Its relations to duende and the blues come to mind.

In short, this textual gem of the heart, mind, soul, and body is an
intellectual feast and existential blues song of he who decided to be
true to his sacred Socratic calling and empty himself of his divine
and human gifts in the open streets of the world to enrich the

precious lives of us all. How blessed I am to have such a sublime Brother in my life!

PROLOGUE

The Wall

Hamlet had it wrong. Life's conundrum is not: to be or not to be. It is: to be and not to be. That is the question, and the answer.

Hamlet was the last mourner of his father's tragic death. All others who claimed to love and grieve over the murdered king had gotten over it and moved on. I am the last mourner of the tragic death of my own father. I will never get over it, though I have moved on, even as time has seemed to stand almost still.

Unlike Hamlet, I have plotted no revenge. Dad would not want me to. I would not want me to. I *do* aim to set certain things to rights, but not by committing further wrongs. I owe it to my dad to do so. More than anyone, he (along with my mother) was the force and the inspiration who made it possible for me—even when he disagreed with my choices—to take on scholarly and professional pursuits that, over time, led me to discover just enough about who I am at my core to dedicate my life to Socrates Café. I launched Socrates Café, a global phenomenon and grassroots movement rolled into one, a quarter century ago as one person's modest yet ambitious contribution toward making ours a more lovable and livable world—in this case, through a form of inclusive inquiry as rigorous and methodical as it is imaginative and even whimsical, at times as exhilarating as it is unsettling, illuminating even as it sometimes muddies things up. A form of inquiry into timely and timeless questions—"Where is love?" "How do you know when you are living an honorable life?" "Why should we seek to improve ourselves?"—in which no one emerges unscathed and most involved feel more "connected" in myriad ways, not just with themselves and one another, but with their society, their world. A form of inquiry in which a primary aim is to make participants, so many of whom live on life's margins, feel seen and heard. A form of inquiry that is the epitome of love.

I'm perched atop a section of the centuries-old cluster of walls of the ancient acropolis, known as the Paleokastro, the crown jewel and erstwhile centerpiece of the diminutive island of Nisyros. One of the chain of insular Dodecanese ("Twelve") islands in the southern Aegean Sea, it is the island from which my grandparents emigrated to the United States—not once, but twice.

The remarkable ruins on the summit of this southeast Aegean island—one of several island groups that include the Cyclades, the Saronic, the North Aegean Island, the Sporades, and Crete—remain among the best-kept archeological secrets. The surrounding sea is an impossibly deep blue at the moment, though it is subject to changes of color without notice as competing weather systems jostle and joust from every direction.

The small volcanic island, with a year-round population of fewer than one thousand, has four villages. My father's family hails from the principal one, Mandraki, where I am staying at an inn owned by relatives. As I make my way from the village to the ancient acropolis, I pass by immaculate agoras, public plazas where to this day, as in Socrates's time, people barter goods as well as exchange ideas and ideals. The agoras are as well kept and dazzling white as the surrounding homes, all made in part of volcanic rocks and insulated with pumice. Once outside the village, I walk along narrow pebble streets and dirt paths that lace their winding way up and through hills and dells before the steep ascent to the acropolis, situated at the highest point—the precise walk that Dad and I had long planned to make together.

I make the climb lost in thought much of the time. But that makes even more breathtaking, whenever I emerge from my reverie, the terraces splashed with bright colors that I pass along the way, featuring a variety of figs, olives, almonds, carobs, prickly pears, flowering cactus. A half hour later, I am at the acropolis. As soon as I reach the plateau, the massive, towering walls of the acropolis come into full view. How forbidding they must have appeared to their would-be besiegers back in the day. A marvel of craftsmanship and design, the parallel outer and inner walls are erected in a way that it is nigh impossible to find a vulnerability by which to penetrate the precisely cut red-hued stone.

At the acropolis, I sit myself on one of its high, wide walls of indestructible volcanic rock. The section of wall on which I plant myself encircles like a stone laurel the acme of the ruins. The ingeniously interlocked walls that protected the ancient fortification remain in pristine enough condition to serve their original purpose in a pinch. Why were such walls needed, not to mention an intricate set of far-flung outposts for sending signals by smoke and fire, devised to provide quick communications? Surely it speaks to the fact that this diminutive, roundish, volcanic island played an outsize role in the infamous long-going fifth-century conflict, the Peloponnesian War. A fair-weather ally, Nisyros was no innocent bystander in the war of wars that led to the demise of the Athenian polis and of Greece as a whole as the central player in more worldly and otherworldly affairs.

With a total surface area of just forty-one kilometers, the island's mostly rocky coastline measures all of twenty-eight kilometers. Nisyros can be reached either by a languorous half-day ferry ride (my choice), from the mainland city of Piraeus, or by boat from one of two nearby islands, Kos or Rhodes, which have small airports with daily flights much of the year to and from Athens. If Greek mythology is to be believed, the island itself came to be as a result of a vengeful and violent act. Once upon a time, Nisyros is said to have been part of the larger island Kos. It came into its own after a fight to the finish between two Titans, Polyvotis and Poseidon. When the giant Polyvotis realized he'd met his match with the Olympian god, he beat a hasty retreat. A furious Poseidon, unable to chase down the fleet-footed Titan, broke off with his trident a piece of Kos and hurled it at Polyvotis. Poseidon's aim was unerring; Polyvotis sank under the weight of the projectile. He's said to be buried to this day underneath what ever since has been Nisyros, the island volcano. The youngest of Greece's six still-active volcanoes (four others are extinct), it still displays sporadic, unmistakable signs of life, though its last full-blown eruptions (three of them) were in the late nineteenth century. Whenever the volcano threatens to come to life in a big way, it is said that Polyvotis is groaning in a Sisyphean effort to writhe and wriggle his way out from underneath the island.

I have been to Nisyros time and again in my mind. In my younger years, I was transported there whenever I pored over a vast collection I'd compiled of books, photographs, even film videos about the island—but most of all by the tales regaled me by my uncle Dimitrios, or Jimmy. He pulled no punches in his colorful, vivid stories of our immediate and extended Nisyrian family, a blend of saints and sinners, do-gooders and do-badders, often all rolled into one.

This is the first time I've physically been on its terra firma. Though I have been to Athens and other parts of mainland Greece during my Socratic sojourns over the years, they were always at times of the year and under circumstances in which a trip to Nisyros remained out of reach. My father and I had long plotted venturing here together after he retired in 1999. During an unforgettable reunion with Dad in the spring of 2011, we laid the detailed groundwork for our trip. It was going to happen at long last.

It was not to be. In mid-September of that year, Dad's life ended. I was never so much as informed of Dad's death (or even that he was in decline) by those with him his final days. When I spoke with one of them, the rationales offered made my blood run cold. One web of blatant contradictions, when I pointed them out, readily morphed into another. I was offered no condolences. To the contrary. Just as chilling was the utter lack of emotion—or rather, if any emotion was conveyed, it was one of snide pleasure, even humor.

What would turn out to be only the latest in a nightmarish chain of events actually started to unfold about a year before my father's death, though I didn't understand this completely until after Dad's funeral; they caused tremendous pain, stress, and sorrow—for no one more than Dad—and at the time of his death and ever since, they have continued to wreak harm and damage. The most sacred promises, confidences, and betrayals of trust were broken, for the most craven ends. They've given me little choice but to open my eyes and see what long had stared me in the face but that I, no more than Dad, would see.

All of a sudden, from the mouth of the island's active volcano— you can actually enter and tour around its otherworldly hypothermal craters—the wind sends my way a bracing whiff of its bubbling sulfur. When will it erupt again? It is little digression to note that to this day, scientists can't predict with any degree of accuracy when a volcano will erupt. Even with global satellites at their disposal to monitor active volcanoes, and even though armed on the ground with intricate networks of state-of-the-art detection instruments, they have no earthly idea when one will awake from its slumber. Professional volcano watchers remain relegated to making best guesses the old-fashioned way, by examining the gas a volcano expels and looking for surface deformations. But because they can't pierce the volcanic rock and soil itself, they have little to no clue whether, much less when, the specific kind of magma that leads to eruptions may be rising to a volcano's surface. What's more, dormant volcanoes often are the picture of quiet and stillness until, with scant warning (if that), the moment arrives that in quantum fashion they erupt with stunning destructive force.

Likewise, a certain kind of human being can for years on end boil inside with rage, and yet go altogether undetected, concealing his fury behind a rock-hard curtain of wiliness, deceit, and most of all charm. Then, without warning, such a person can blow his top. Some months before his death, my father shared with me that he had someone under his wing whom he'd rescued from one debacle after another. When Dad yet again bailed out this person, he related that he then administered a lecture about the immoral cupidity of duping innocent people into shelling out their hard-earned money in get-rich-quick schemes and scams. Dad told me that, all of a sudden, without the slightest warning, this person exploded at him. The eruption was tamped down only when, with trembling hands, Dad said he managed to open his flip phone and threatened to call the police. I did not act on what Dad shared, no more than he took precautions to stay safer. At the time, we didn't see what was what, much less what was coming, even though in retrospect there were evident signs of anger-fueled deterioration, even on the surface. Just as with physical volcanoes, human eruptions can happen with unexpected swiftness and destructiveness. After it has passed, you convince yourself that's the end of it. Yet anyone who has studied volcanoes of any sort knows that they can erupt in many different ways, and that the initial spectacular burst can be followed by a series of "quieter" ones that nonetheless exact far more damage—and woe betide those on the receiving end.

I spoke to Dad by phone several days before his life ended. From the tenor and tremor of his voice, and from what he did—and didn't—say, he appeared frightened and resigned. I told him I would drop everything I had scheduled—I was in the midst of an intensive book tour and series of presentations—and come there at once. Gallant to a fault, Dad then said, in a stronger voice that sounded more like himself, that I needed to stick with my commitments. "I'll be okay. You have a young family to support," he said. "Come see me in a couple weeks."

"I love you," I said.

"I love *you*," he said. That's how Dad always replied—"I love *you*"—whenever I was the first of us to say those three words: "I love *you*."

Those were the last words we ever exchanged. I treasure them beyond measure.

THE WALL THAT BRIDGES

All my life, whether rooted in one place for lengthy periods, as I was in my younger years, or whether a rolling stone, as I have been most of my adult years (even at times after marrying and having a family), I have never felt entirely at home, never felt I belonged—*atopos*, the Greeks of old called this feeling. Here on this island, at last, I have arrived. Home at last. I belong. While untold numbers of people have occupied the perch where I am right now on this acropolis wall, I can say with certainty that, right now, it belongs to me. It is my space on my wall. This is for me an Odyssey-like homecoming to a Greek island's rocky shores after a long existential shipwreck.

I am one with the grand and not so grand scheme of things, in a way I've never before experienced. I am at home straddling realms, with the squishiness of time and space. Here at last I feel a sense of place, and of inner and outer belonging. I can't say this has brought me peace, but I am no longer so unmoored, no longer so roiling on the inside. I now know what it is to be anchored and untethered, at one and the same time, like an existential trapeze artist.

I exist in sea time right now.

Surrounded by the Aegean, the waters that strike the coast are more or less the same. There is an air of changelessness, of unending departure and return. Surely one day it will be discovered that time has both infinite progress and regress. One of the earliest English versions of the phrase "Time and tide waits for no one," in the thirteenth century, goes: "The tide abides for, tarrieth for no man, stays no man, tide nor time tarrieth no man." Geoffrey Chaucer writes in his prologue to *The Clerk's Tale*, published in 1395, "For though we sleep, or wake, or roam, or ride, the time will fly; it will pause for no man." In its earliest iteration, tide meant noontide—noon or midday. Yet it still has to do with *tide* tides, how we humans are inexorably caught up both in the passage of time as well the movements of the tides.

All too many live as if they have all the time in the world. Even when the holy grail is at last hit upon—it will be sooner than later, mark my words—that keeps our cells from aging, a development that will vastly extend the lives of so many of my species, especially the more well off, all it might portend is that most people will have even more years to fritter away.

Born and raised along the large, sweeping Warwick River in Virginia, I spent countless hours along it, and afloat in it in our family boat—fishing, catching crabs, conversing with the gods, escaping family turmoil, contemplating. I was well aware even in those days that, among the fragments that have been discovered of the writings of the pre-Socratic philosopher Heraclitus, is this: "No man ever steps in the same river twice, for it's not the same river and he's not the same man." In the case of the sea, however, you do step into it twice and thrice, ad infinitum. It's essentially the same and essentially not—ebb and flow, evolution and devolution, rise and fall, an approaching and a retreat.

I have been fascinated by the sheer heights and depths and expansiveness of feelings and emotions and thoughts that have wended their way through me since Dad's life ended in a way that made it impossible for us to say our goodbyes. Fascinated not in a narcissistic or a morbid manner, but rather by the sheer mortifying shock of what happened to Dad and the withering reprisals to which I have since been subjected.

Upon learning of my father's tragic death in a manner that was beyond abysmal and mortifying, I was left reeling. I was caught unawares, unprepared and ill equipped to deal with the ensuing onslaught of machinations to which I was subjected.

Or so I thought.

In the wake of Dad's death, in spite of periodic waves of stultifying, overwhelming sorrow, I have gone on to be named the first senior educational fellow at the vaunted National Constitution Center, I was appointed an ethics fellow at Harvard University, I was recipient of the Distinguished American Leadership Award, I went on to write several new philosophical works for adults and for children, I was made a senior research and writing fellow at another Ivy League university; I established a new global initiative called Democracy Café, a complement to Socrates Café, that has brought together people the world over both to explore and take concrete action for realizing more open societies and selves on myriad scales—and best of all, I became a dad again, to a true bundle of empathy and joy, Cybele (named after the Greek goddess of nature and healing).

In spite of all the heartbreak, I have since come to discover that I'm made of stronger and sterner stuff than I'd given myself credit for. I attribute it in large part to my "Socratic spirit." The seeds of this spirit were sown by the intimidating and inspiring insistence of Dad's mother, my *yaya*, my Greek grandmother Calliope Kavazarakis Philipou. She initiated me into a world of works by Sophocles, Aeschylus, Homer, Euripides, and most of all Plato.

My *yaya* was the first independent teacher-entrepreneur of Greek language and culture in the Tampa Bay region. She put out her shingle after she, her husband—my namesake Philip (Philip Dimitrios Philipou)—and their three children settled in Tampa in 1935. My summer vacations were spent there, often under her wing, the original helicopter and tiger grandmother. They were the furthest thing from the typical, more leisure-like (certainly less studious) summer breathers enjoyed by the peers I left behind in Virginia. For me, these times away from the formal, hallowed halls were occasion to be schooled intensively and extensively by my *yaya*, a Hellenophile to end all Hellenophiles.

Her birthday gift to me one young year, of a handsomely bound copy of Plato's Socratic dialogues, was not without motive; it was pretext for her youngest grandson to pore over, first and foremost, Plato's *Apology*. She tweaked my cheek with loving, painful force as she handed over the gift. "You are the one who will be like his protagonist, Socrates," she said. How could Yaya have been so sure? It would turn out that no piece of literature, fiction or nonfiction, poetry or drama, has touched me like the Socrates of Plato's *Apology*. Here was a human who did it his way, through days of glory and, even more so, days of opprobrium and scapegoating, all in the name of realizing a more exalted type of excellent life for one and all.

I, of course, was moved in the *Apology* by what is widely considered Socrates's most memorable assertion, that "the unexamined life is not worth living." On the other hand, that seemed a no-brainer—what child of my age at that time doesn't have it in his or her DNA to examine without cease life in all its dimensions? What struck me most in that real-life drama of Plato's capturing Socrates's final hours was the septuagenarian's insistence to those present with him at the end that they should "understand that I shall never alter my ways, not even if I have to die many times." Socrates was asserting so much more than his celebrated platitude that the unexamined life is not worth living. His revolutionary declaration here was: the examined life is worth dying for.

Behold a human, bundled into an unhandsome exterior package of a pug-nosed man with an ill-kempt beard and questionable taste in clothes and some of his intimates. A human who was not to be deterred or derailed in his quest for honest insight into how to achieve human excellence in all its dimensions. A man filled with a joy that emerges on the other side of agony, betrayal, despair.

How could he be so free of resentment? The closest Socrates came to a lament of the obscene unjustness of the orchestration of his death sentence was just before he took his life: "In another world they do not put a man to death for asking questions: assuredly not." Even that was without bitterness or self-pity of the maudlin sort displayed by Job of the Old Testament. Instead of asking, "Why me?" in woe-is-me fashion like Job, Socrates left it at, "Why not me?" In this spirit, he was bound and determined even (especially) on the cusp of ending his life to chart new beginnings for those he left behind.

Socrates was the real deal, an unstoppable force of human nature. He wasn't *more* than human, he wasn't larger than life, but rather he was a living, breathing example of how to go about living and dying that serves as a beacon, as well as a cautionary tale, of how little most of us humans settle for.

Socrates was spirit personified—not spiritual (a term that has come to mean so many things it means next to nothing), but spirited, spirit filled, of the sort out of which the Hellenic Greek concept of human *arete*—what the Greek scholar H. D. F. Kitto refers to as the unending quest to become an excellent all-rounder—is brewed and realized. Nothing could break the man. As the target of the most repugnant acts, he redoubled his efforts to do what he could while he could to heal Athens—not as a proselytizer or a messiah, but as an unflinching inquirer determined to discover still more about the "life of should." He did not do so as a pure dyed-in-the-wool rationalist, but as someone with a decided poetic dimension, even a tinge of madness and healthy doses of intoxication, all ingredients for imagining and experimenting with new possibilities for life and living.

Actually, Socrates was a constellation of spirits. Just as Virtue is made of virtues, the fifth-century BC philosopher himself is Spirit composed of spirits. In my latter childhood years, immersing myself in Plato's dialogues and also attempting to spearhead such dialogues myself—with family, friends, at school, as much a way of communing with Socrates (and myself) as anything else—I started to see the ancient interrogator as a living, breathing concatenation of spirits. In all the years since, in which I've taken a stab at carrying the Socratic torch, I'm more convinced than ever that he was an amalgam of: *daimon, atopos, eudaimonia, sophrosyne*. All in the name of *arete*, to achieve a higher kind of *sophia*, or wisdom—both of which are not spirits themselves, but the results of what certain spirits can achieve for a self and a society (which is a kind of self) when they are operating at their optimum. And all of which can only be accomplished if you have a healthy soul, a soul of goodness.

Here's how I described my tentative or preliminary "findings" on the matter in 1971, one summer in Tampa, Florida, where I made an enforced but rewarding pilgrimage from my hometown of Newport News, Virginia, each and every protracted vacation of my life until age eighteen. That preteen summer of 1971, I presented to Yaya a booklet. Bound with knitting yarn tied through three holes punched in the left margin, it was titled *The Spirits of Arete*. It had a cover design featuring a Venn diagram of Socrates's spirits.

Inside, I wrote in my inimitable excited scrawl:

—*Daimon*—Divine voice of conscience, reflection, self-awareness, goodness. "You have often heard me speak of an oracle or sign which comes to me, and is the divinity. . . . This sign I have had ever since I was a child."—Socrates, Plato's *Apology*

—*Atopos*—Spirit of a wanderer rooted at home, apart from yet connected, out of place yet belonging, strange yet familiar, marvelous and distasteful. Agathon, Plato's *Gorgias*—"This is a custom of [Socrates]: . . . he stands apart wherever he happens to be."

—*Eudaimonia*—Guarantor of human flourishing, wellness, prosperity, blessedness. Spirit of joy obtained through suffering and agony, when your heart is in another. "The one who lives well"—for *arete*—is blessed, prosperous and joyful.— Socrates, Plato's *Republic*, Book 1

—*Sophrosyne*—Spirit of a sound and healthy (good and just) mind and soul. Conductor of the spirit orchestra. Teaches you when to restrain and when to let loose, when to go it alone and when to team up. Socrates, Plato's *Republic*, Book 4: "*Sophrosyne* . . . stretches through the whole, from top to bottom of the entire scale, making the weaker, the stronger, and those in the middle . . . sing the same chant together."

It is the chant of *arete*. A siren song with *sophia*-scored notes, compelling you to lead a life outside common hours, marching to your own drummer. It does not lead one to set out to achieve the comparatively puny goals of happiness or the good life—goals commonly and scandalously misattributed to Socrates himself—but leads one to reach for kinds of excellence and joyousness on the other side of (or more likely, along with) suffering, agony, despair.

The spirits that Socrates harbored within as he engaged in inquiries without made him a matchless force to be reckoned with in the name of realizing, and at the same time expanding, the possibilities for *arete* and the *sophia* interweaved with it. Not even the hardest knocks, the thousand natural shocks and then some, that came his way could keep this good man down. His spirit was of the shatterproof variety.

With Socrates as my inspirational guide, I was readying myself—unbeknownst to me in that long-ago time—for the day when a concerted attempt, carried out with malevolent intent, was made to break my own spirit.

In those days, I made early attempts at inquiry à la Socrates. One of them was a spontaneous query I made at a family Thanksgiving dinner shortly after an argument broke out. My mother had slaved away all day at preparing a delectable meal, and my father and older brother wanted to fill their plates and eat in the family room while glued to the TV set watching an NFL football game. Mom was upset, and rightfully so. Thanksgiving was about togetherness, after all. She was not met with the understanding one might expect. An argument—never dialogue, always argument—ensued. I blurted out, "Why is family togetherness important?" I then sat at the table with my meal, served buffet-style, and began to eat in thoughtful silence. Everyone else filled their plates and sat down, one by one. The question itself brought us together at the table, and for a brief while, we enjoyed our Thanksgiving meal in one another's company. Later we had popcorn and played Jeopardy in the family room while football was on TV. Even questions posed and unanswered sometimes can work a certain magic.

On another occasion, when I was about fourteen, in the height of the school desegregation era, I was bused each weekday at 6:00 a.m. to a decrepit middle school on the other side of Newport News. I'd recently read a book on race by anthropologist Ashley Montagu—a Socratic type if ever there was one who challenged the received wisdom of the day on race matters—that made the case that the concept of race for all intents and purposes didn't exist from a biological standpoint. It struck me that we might be better off doing away with race as a social concept as well, given how it has fanned so much racist vitriol and violence since time immemorial. At the school cafeteria one day, I plopped myself between black students on one side and white students on the other, and I asked, "What would a world without race be like?" Once again, I was met with silence. Then an imposing white student dumped chocolate and white milk on my tray and said, "It's kinda like that," before walking away. The rest stayed put, looking at me with faces that seemed to convey, "That kid's got some balls." A popular black athlete finally chimed in: "There is some of that 'race-free world' on our football team. But not in my family." Trey shared that his sister was going steady with a white schoolmate, and now no one in his family talked to her. A white student then offered that his black friends expanded his horizons when it came to things like music and food, books and magazines. He thought some more: "Most of all, you're influenced by whomever you hang out with," he then said. "I have a culture, or cultures—my family, my friends, the people in the clubs I belong to and sports teams I participate in, my church. I sometimes wished there were more people living in this city from different cultures and ethnic groups, like there were when I lived in New York City. But there is a different kind of diversity here, and I celebrate that. My parents raised me by Martin Luther King Jr.'s belief that you judge people by the content of their character, not the color of their skin. So race is the least consideration for me when I decide who to hang out with."

I'm not sure I ever said a word after throwing out the question. Lunch only lasted twenty-five minutes. Most amazing to me was that students who usually had nothing to do with one another were talking among themselves without being overly self-conscious about it. When I was in the hallway alone later in the afternoon, the hulking white student who wanted nothing to do with my dialogue and had tried to humiliate me waylaid me; he told me if I ever pulled "a stunt like that" again, he'd break my arm—and he twisted it back painfully, to show me he meant it. When he let go, quicker than thought, I wheeled around and punched him in the nose with everything I had. His nose gushed blood. I was aghast and ashamed. I apologized. "Are you okay?" He shook me off, and backed off. He made his way to the infirmary. I went in tow even as he kept trying to brush me away. He told the nurse he'd slipped. He never told a soul what really happened, and for whatever reason never tried to get retribution. Though I have never hit anyone again, ever since then, I've known what I'm capable of. Just as, on a more positive note, that lunchtime experience at my middle school made me realize I was capable of orchestrating philosophical music among unlikely bedfellows.

Nietzsche writes in his *Birth of Tragedy* that Socrates was the exemplar of a person imbued with the spirit of *sophrosyne*:

> Even the most sublime ethical deeds, the stirrings of pity, self-sacrifice, heroism, of that calm sea of the soul, so difficult to attain, which the Apollinian Greek called *sophrosyne*, were derived from the dialectic of knowledge by Socrates and his like-minded successors, down to the present, and accordingly designated as teachable.

What Socrates managed to do, as Nietzsche notes here (for once in understated fashion), was "teachable." His method and ethos of philosophical inquiry, though not at all easy, could be practiced by most anyone anywhere who was willing to attempt the feat in similar ways for similar ends in one's own time and clime. As far as I know, it's the only way to cultivate the spirits of Socrates. You can't do it just by poring over his works in a scholarly fashion, though that, of course, can be a complement and impetus.

To discover more about *arete*, you have to practice it. *Arete* in action is the rigorous and relentless practice of Socratic inquiry in order to achieve kinds of wisdom that are interlaced with moral imagination and social conscience. It's how you develop and fortify the Socratic spirits, the spirits of *arete*, much like a feedback loop. There are no shortcuts, and there is no final destination. It's how you sculpt the goodness and healthiness of soul that can withstand (or has the best chance of withstanding) life's most extreme slings and arrows.

Those "like-minded successors" Nietzsche lauds have been the remnant who—ever since Socrates's death, through inquiring themselves in the same vein he did and for the same objectives—have experienced highs (and lows) that can only be had from cultivating and mastering themselves these spirits. "Anyone who has had the pleasure of Socratic insight . . . spreading in ever-widening circles," Nietzsche writes, is experiencing "an altogether new form of 'Greek cheerfulness' and blissful affirmation of existence that seeks to discharge itself in actions." You must have the chutzpah to act on your hard-won insights. By doing so, that orchestra leader of the spirits—*sophrosyne*, a.k.a. "Greek cheerfulness"—that conspires and collaborates with the other spirits of *arete*, is in turn further shaped and molded. It leads to more gracefulness and graciousness of manner and spirit in living, overcoming, and understanding, no matter what comes one's way, in the worst of times even more than in the best.

WALL WITH EYES

Another invisible sulfurous wave wafts my way from the volcano entrance below. It is not unpleasant. If anything, it's intoxicating. For anyone who asserts that Socrates was the epitome of rationality, one need only counter that his mission in life arose from his pilgrimage to the oracle of Delphi, a priestess, mystic, and seer—no one's idea of a purely reasoning being—who more often than not was in a trancelike state.[1] When the oracle issued to Socrates the curt but irresistible charge, "Know thyself," he at once accepted it, if not unquestioningly, then wholeheartedly—it spoke to his lost soul—and for the remainder of his life he sought and found himself, again and again, through inquiry with others, like no other.

Scientists have recently discovered that the oracle's shrine was a hotbed of vaporous, gaseous emissions that arose from the many chasms, fault lines, and fissures throughout her temple, and which produced a euphoric, near-hypnotic state in her and those in her company. I can't say for certain that I am having a similar experience as Socrates, but I can attest that it is at the apex of this volcanic island (more accurate would be to call Nisyros itself an active volcano), about seven hundred meters above sea level, as I inhale the volcano's seductive vapors, that the wall between the living and its converse, between the real and its antitheses, between tenses themselves, dissolves for me like so many desiccated bones exposed to the sun for years beyond count.

Nisyros is the land, the place, I have been looking for most all of my life. This wall I'm on, it turns out, is also a bridge—to those here who came before me and who will come after me, and most of all to my father. Call it momentary madness if you like, but if so, it does not feel unhealthy or untoward. Hamlet saw his own father's spirit pacing along a castle wall. In my case, with an ineffable intensity of feeling and vision, my own father is sitting right here beside me. Excited and giddy like a kid, Dad's off-white tennis shoes bounce off the side of the wall on which we're perched. At this precise moment, I am as one with Shakespeare's sensibility that when certain acts are committed, the spirit of the person who was on the receiving end of those acts may linger after death.

"Peace, peace! he is not dead, he doth not sleep—He hath awakened from the dream of life." This passage from Percy Bysshe Shelley's *Adonais*—a stirring elegy by the Romantic philosophical poet, penned while grieving over his young friend, fellow poet John Keats, who died in untimely and tragic fashion—emerges unbidden. Maybe the least likely passage you'd expect me or anyone else to utter on an ancient wall on a pip-squeak of a Greek island. Shelley himself is, among other things, evoking the grieving Hamlet's encounter with his father's spirit. This poem long has been part of my existential DNA. What I can't tell is whether I'm saying the words out loud or just moving my lips along to them.

Since Dad's death, I have had any number of vivid conversations with him, many unbidden, in sleeping and waking moments. At this moment, though, at the heights of Nisyros, neither of us feels a need or desire to speak. From my—our—elevated vantage point, it's possible to survey the entire panorama of the sea and what are now near-endless shades of blue and green. Far out and below, the white foam of the Aegean Sea crashes against craggy rocks that abut promontories and steep cliffs, where seagulls fly and screech overhead in erratic circles. The waves breaking along the coast from almost all directions make a faint yet audible sound akin to a sustained, modulated roar.

At least for the moment, my heart is no longer so shattered, my soul not so fragmented. Until the death of my father, Alexander Phillips, née Alexandros Philipou, I had taken it for granted that my immediate orbit was, by and large, a rational and sensible one, that those inhabiting it had at least some degree of moral compass. That assumption has crashed and burned. I had been blind. Blind to malady, malignance, malevolence, festering over decades, at last manifesting itself with a vindictive cunning that nearly broke me, the shock and disbelief still at times staggering.

To see and not to see.

Was I a willful practitioner of blindness?

You see what you want or choose to. You see what you don't want or choose to. You see what isn't there, and don't see what is. Fears, of both the rational and irrational variety, play a part. As do love and devotion.

So easy to see even the most minute flaws and hard truths in others, so hard to detect even the most magnified ones in yourself.

Socrates journeyed to visit the oracle residing at the temple of Apollo in the village of Delphi to which most Greeks of his era flocked. After his encounter there with her, her exhortation, "Know thyself," became his mission in life. But what is left unacknowledged is that knowing yourself doesn't mean, as a matter of course, that the self you discover will facilitate your moving forward and upward in life. It doesn't necessarily set you free from self- or other-imposed shackles. The self with whom you come face-to-face might set you back, prompt you to wish you'd never set out on the journey in the first place. It might demolish your spirit, crush you with guilt. The self-knowledge gleaned by Sophocles's Oedipus laid waste to his hubristic notion that he was the wisest of all, and led to his ruin by his own hand.

It doesn't have to be that way.

The Socrates Café–goers I've had the privilege to encounter long have served as gentle mirrors into my inner- and outermost public and private selves. My investigations with them have laid bare hypocrisies and contradictions, as well as exposed merits and virtues to which I otherwise wouldn't have been privy. Thanks to them, I've been able to come face-to-face with defects in my character that would have held me back on the road to *arete*. Even so, I have discovered blinders and blind spots of mine that in hindsight are gaping and glaring—and when you do become aware of them, it can shake and shock you to the core. My father's death, and the truths I have had to unearth and confront, have turned upside down so much of what I thought I knew about myself and those around me.

WALL FOR TEARS

I erupt in tears. An outpouring of anguish. I rock back and forth on the wall, a rumbling moan coming from an unrecognizable place deep inside.

I get it out of my system at last.

Because of my nature, similar in this respect to Dad's, even in my deep grief, I'm struck by a wave of gratitude. Dad lived to see my Socrates Café initiative, and several of my books about my rich experiences "Socratizing" with people of all ages and walks of life, garner acclaim among both popular and scholarly audiences (he prized scholarship) the world over, and best of all in his beloved Greece. He was a Hellenophile to the nth degree. Besides being a lifelong member of the Nisyrian Society, which celebrates all things bright and beautiful about the island of his roots, Dad served for years as chapter president in Newport News, Virginia, of the American Hellenic Education Progressive Association, or AHEPA. The oldest and largest organization in the U.S. of its kind, AHEPA advances the ancient Greek ideals and virtues of education for democratic citizenship; civic responsibility and service; and the blended cultivation of individual, family, and societal excellence (of *arete*, in a word). Founded in the U.S. in 1922, the same year my grandparents arrived here (for the first time) via Ellis Island, AHEPA's original purpose was to counter the extensive racism and virulent bigotry against Greeks spearheaded by Ku Klux Klan members and their like.

Dad also lived to see me gain Greek citizenship. My application made its way through the labyrinthine channels of Greece's bureaucracy at a record pace, according to the consulate at the Greek embassy in Washington, D.C., where I'd submitted mountains of supporting paperwork, including a moving letter from the president of the Nisyrian Society tracing my family's rich history of contributions to the best in our heritage both in Greece and in the U.S. Usually a yearslong process with an uncertain outcome, in my case, just a few months after I made my application, I found myself giving my citizenship oath in a ceremony at the Greek embassy in our nation's capital. "Your *yaya* and your *pappous*, after whom you're named, would be so proud," Dad had said, his voice breaking. "You've brought our family full circle."

I agreed at the time. Yet how do you bring full circle any family, immediate or extended, in which some are separated, or separate themselves, by unscalable walls and unbridgeable moats? Odds are that any of us who has read the chronicles of John Cheever's suburbia and its leafy, manicured, middle-class neighborhoods, and who has grown up himself in such surroundings, has experienced to some degree a real-life version of his fiction. Cheever's tales expose what goes on behind closed doors of many of the homes in those environs—sparkling, landscaped homes inside of which some inhabitants' lives are made dull, consumed by bottomless pettiness, senseless jealousies, resentments, and worse. His stories also relate, with an insider's knowledge, the explosive internecine conflicts in these cloisters.

Cheever captures unsettling truths of the residents' dissembling images and professed values, which clash with their truer, darker, more concealed natures. It is this irreconcilable inner friction that at times can prompt them to lash out at and judge others with hypocritical stridence. Cheever also nails on the head the destructive conflicts among siblings. The author's older brother suffered from alcoholism and depression. Rightly or wrongly, Cheever was convinced that he himself was the cause of this. His brother, he recalls, "was happy, high-spirited, and adored," until he, the little brother, arrived on the scene. Cheever says his brother's "forebodings would naturally have been bitter and deep . . . violent and ambiguous—hatred and love."

Rather than partitioning human sentiments, Cheever unpacks them, teases out searing revelations, refusing to oversimplify or distill the entwined emotions of deep-rooted resentment and love, fierce envy and protectiveness. The imprisoning confines of middle-class existence were the petri dish from which he culls truths about the human condition, and the conditioning of humans.

I made a precocious vow to myself to set myself free from my own "Cheeverian" web, and to live by my own set of evolving expectations, morality, ends. I didn't do this as some holier-than-thou attempt to place myself above or beyond those who had no will to or interest in escape. Nonetheless, I did begin to conceive of an exit strategy. Through the journey of reading timeless works, of thinking and communing with characters real and fictional, I imagined for myself taking a different trajectory in life.

I do not agree with the existentialists, no more than Socrates would have, that man's lot is one in which we are doomed to die. Rather, we are sentenced to live; and what matters most, for those of us fortunate enough to be in a position to do so, is to make the most of this time of ours as mortals, give the gift and curse of life everything we have, no matter how little or much time we're allotted or the hand we're dealt.

In that long-ago time, I became all too aware of the propensity among many to "do as I say, not as I do." Even when quite young, I made it a point to be conscious of whether my words and deeds were in sync, and when they were not, to bring them into unison as much as I could. I was influenced in part by a fragment from the pre-Socratic philosopher Heraclitus of Ephesus, who makes the claim that "a man's character is his fate." Even from a fragment like this, one gleans that Heraclitus's emphasis on man's nature, man's lot, man's character was of the nonformulaic, one-size-does-*not*-fit-all sort. It is not nearly sufficient, no matter what some Sophists and Stoics claim, to *train* our characters to somehow be ready for what one can never be ready for—the most inconceivable slings and arrows, agonies and tragedies. What one *can* do is cultivate one's spirits, so that in the event they do come your way, you just might be able to confront them, absorb them, channel them in ways that just might make us stronger, at least for a while.

Better put: a man's words and works and deeds *are* his character, determining his fate and that of many others. This notion sprung in large part from my readings at a young age of Plato's *Laches*, one of the earlier dialogues that most scholars agree is a faithful representation of Socrates's historical give-and-take. Socrates and Laches arrive at the conclusion that when one's words are not in alignment or in harmony with one's deeds, it can be evidence of a lack of courage—and hypocrisy. Yet few of us bring into complete alignment our words and deeds. Sometimes, as we strive to do so, we discover—through further reflection and the sheer accumulation of more experiences that require still more reflection—that the aims we had aspired for aren't all they were cracked up to be; as a consequence, we amend or overhaul them.

Philosophy itself isn't just a bunch of talk, as Socrates knew better than anyone, but a way of doing and being. In his *Memorabilia*, Xenophon, the noted historian of antiquity as well as student and protégé of Socrates, says that his mentor asserted, "If I don't reveal my views in a formal account, I do so by my conduct." Socrates then asked more than rhetorically: "Don't you think that actions are more reliable evidence than words?" Words, of course, are a spoken or uttered form of conduct. But Socrates is stressing that if our actual deeds in the professional and private spheres do not mirror the things we say, then it makes a mockery of both. In his view, your words—what you say—as well your works—what you make—*and* your deeds—what you do—reveal who you are.

As a child and teen, I attended Greek Orthodox church services, was a member of the Fellowship of Christian Athletes and the Royal Ambassadors (a Christian version of the Boy Scouts, of which I also was a member). To this day, among the readings in which I immersed myself in those days from the Old and New Testaments that have stayed with me ever since are those of the prophets Jeremiah and Ezekiel. They were "Socratic," daring to call out soothsayers and sophists, especially those in positions of power, whose words and deeds, to the detriment of most others, didn't match up. Jeremiah's scathing indictment of the false prophets of his day still rings in my ears: "They have healed the wound of my people lightly, saying, 'Peace, peace' when there is no peace" (Jer. 6:14 ESV). Ezekiel also declaims "false prophets" who "lead my people astray, saying, 'Peace' when there is no peace." With their seductive, specious reassurances, false prophets are like fraudulent buildings who "when a flimsy wall is built, they cover it with whitewash" (Ezek. 13:10 NIV) to give it the fake appearance of sturdiness.

To Socrates, as with Jeremiah and Ezekiel, you must do your utmost to see to it that your words match your deeds—not as an end in itself, but as a condition for achieving *arete*. Saying, doing, making—all that we've wrought—should be directed toward, as he puts it in the *Apology*, an all-out effort to "fighting for the right," whether you live a long time or you "live even for a brief space."

Socrates put his existential money where his mouth was as a private citizen, but also during his brief tenure in public office. As he relates, he refused to be part of "the sort of commands" issued by the corrupt Thirty Tyrants—the pro-Spartan oligarchy that was installed after Athens lost the Peloponnesian War in 404 BC—in "which they were always given with the view of implicating as many as possible in their crimes." Socrates would have none of it. Better to die. "I showed," Socrates recounts, "not in word only but in deed, that . . . I cared not a straw for death, and that my great and only care was lest I should do an unrighteous or unholy thing. For the strong arm of that oppressive power did not frighten me into doing wrong." Socrates was ready to die then and there rather than act in a way in which his comportment contradicted his professed values.

This raises the question: How do you discover which values you should hold most dear? Socrates's answer: by continual exchanges of ideas and ideals, virtues and values and visions, with others, and by subjecting them to "testing" with actual attempts at putting them into practice. It is how you discover ever more about what ethical colors to sail under. Most everyone at some point preaches to himself and others what he does not yet practice (and maybe never will practice, sometimes for good reason). Likewise, from time to time most everyone acts in or on the world in ways that are contradictory or inconsistent with the views they profess. But inquiry of a Socratic kind can enable conscientious individuals to discover hypocrisies and contradictions they'd been unaware of, and inspire them to further bridge the gap between what they say, what they make, what they do.

By the time Socrates was sentenced to death, the age of the sage had been supplanted by the age of rage. The greedier people became, the more they sated their greed, crossing any moral line to do so, the angrier they became. Just as is the case in our own gilded age, people discovered boundless material wealth wasn't the pot of gold at the end of the rainbow they'd expected. Too often, more like fool's gold in an abyss of their making. This "discovery" stoked even greater sound and fury, signifying discord and dissension and, in the case of Athens, marking its death knell. The chasm between word and deed became more and more gaping as a widespread pathology took hold. It wasn't that a dark wall of night was oncoming. It had already come.

WALL OF A SEER

The original purpose of the centuries-old wall of the Nisyrian acropolis may long ago have gone by the wayside, but on a clear day like today, you can see, from its unique position between the Eastern and Western worlds (and the northern and southern for that matter) far off into the distance in every direction. If you sit here long enough, it might make a seer of you; it may give you little choice but to see that another wall of night is fast approaching.

All the more reason, in my estimation, to "live like Socrates." To do that, you no more live like there's no tomorrow than you live in a way that fulfills Macbeth's lamentation that "tomorrow, and tomorrow, and tomorrow" are devoid of meaning. A predominant theme of Sartre's 1939 short story "The Wall," set in Spain during the just-ended Spanish Civil War, is that those who know they face impending death—like the three brigade members in the story who are captured by Franco's troops and slated to be shot in the morning—are partitioned from the rest of the living because of their intensely painful awareness of their all-too-soon meeting with their maker. The protagonist Pablo finds solace in the certainty that his jailers and interrogators themselves will die not long from now. Yet Pablo, it turns out, through a ruse with an unexpected outcome, lives to see another day and meet with a different fate than the others in his cell who are put to death the following day. Sometimes you think your time is up, and against all odds, it isn't. Sometimes you have every reason to think you have a long life ahead of you, only for it to be cut short. You never know. What matters are your works and deeds, in whatever amount of time you have. They count, they matter, from here to eternity and back.

THE GOOD, THE BAD, AND THE UGLY

Socrates pontificated about the kinds of walls that human societies tend to construct in order to put themselves over and above others. He was well aware, from a multitude of firsthand experiences and encounters, of the good, the bad, and the ugly purposes such walls can serve. In his time, a certain kind of wall built by Athenians and by Spartans, each in their own right, was an enabler for extreme jingoism. As a result, each convinced themselves that they had might and right exclusively on their respective side. The warring Greek tribes went after one another with hammer and tongs in the protracted Peloponnesian conflict, both equally petty, rash, suspicious, misguided, noble, virtuous, and brave as hell.

What each side lacked was the critical self-awareness and honesty needed to see its own badness and ugliness. Each only had eyes for the vices in the other, and eyes only for its own goodness and greatness. The twenty-seven-year-long Peloponnesian War itself is evidence of this. It was triggered by a perceived slight by the Athenians; they'd offered Sparta their assistance in a conflict it was in the thick of, and were rejected. Not to be outdone, the Spartans later felt dissed when Athens abetted a tribe of Greeks that they considered opponents. Both overreacted in like fashion, and their spat morphed into all-out war. Athens considered itself unbeatable. Its citizens' true colors were revealed when its military undertook not just to trounce Sparta in the war itself, but to engage in a naked all-out grab for its land and resources.

Bettany Hughes notes in her critically praised *The Hemlock Cup: Socrates, Athens and the Search for the Good Life*, that "Socrates was acutely aware of the dangers of excess and overindulgence. . . . He berated his peers for a selfish pursuit of material gain. He questioned the value of going to fight under an ideological banner of 'democracy.'"

Socrates was not in any way opposed to material possessions; but he believed that if it became the paramount or sole end—if most everyone was on the take, stuffing their pockets with ill-gotten gain—it would be a harbinger that Athens' ascent as a creative, probing, participatory society would be stopped in its tracks and ultimately derailed, the handwriting on the wall.

Which is what happened.

Socrates also knew that physical walls could be at cross-purposes. Despite intentions, such walls can entrap a people from within, rather than serve their aim and protect them from external dangers. During Athens' conflict with Sparta, in which Socrates put himself in harm's way as an infantryman, the encircling physical wall of Athens was meant to guard its denizens from outside aggressors. Instead, it bottled up and spread a plague, decimating the population—a development that made the Athenians' eventual defeat a foregone conclusion.

Socrates's optimistic, faith-driven premise about humans, as he puts it in *Protagoras*, was that "no one does wrong willingly." His inquiries aimed to shed light on how to do right knowingly. His unshakable belief was that once you're able to recognize when and how you're doing wrong, you'll do your utmost to do right willingly instead. Most of his fellow Athenians, though, belied this in their decline. They'd become afflicted by ethical pestilence—what might best be called an incurable case of pot-calling-the-kettle-blackism. They accused others of what they themselves had become. With its citizenry blind to its own failings, Athens failed.

Or is that too simplistic? Are things often, if not most always, messier than that? As I sit on this still-intact wall—a wall that has outlived and outlasted its purpose, the acropolis buildings inside now long buried well below, still waiting to be excavated—I wonder: How is it that a moral—or better put, *a*moral—contagion could take hold among a populace like that of Athens that long had strived for excellence in such a playful, creative, collaborative and competitive, persistent, and upward-moving way? Were the makings of this much longer in the works than meets the eye? Or was it some sort of spontaneous implosion that punctuated their long-sustained, ever-ascending moral equilibrium? What kinds of circumstances might compel many or most of even the best-intentioned people, as individuals and a collective, to take a dramatic turn for the worst? Can a chance event here, another one there, trigger a sea change in conduct and the values that drive a citizenry? What about the plague that struck Athenians, after their decision to wall themselves in from any would-be besiegers? Did it not only have the precise opposite impact on them physically—trapping them within, facilitating the plague's spread, wiping out their population—but morally as well? After the plague, allies became enemies, and enemies allies. On a more intimate scale, members of families, of neighborhoods, of the polis, became pitted against one another. Was its individual and collective wiring always susceptible to such a turn of events?

Such thoughts of mine oscillate between and among musings about my own family, past and present (and future), from this place where our story in many ways began. How can it be that decent people can break bad, break diabolical, even at a late stage in life? Were the signs there all along? What role is played by wiring, by genetic makeup? How does circumstance or happenstance, the forces we contend with and that contend with us, factor in? How about nurture or lack thereof, or if any of those charged with providing nurture are themselves irretrievably damaged from their own upbringing?

MAY THE FORCE BE WITH YOU

The French philosopher, mystic, and humanitarian activist Simone Weil's provocative thought piece, *L'Iliade ou le poème de la force*—"The Iliad, or The Poem of Force"—published in 1940 about the eighth-century BC epic poem by Homer, holds that "the true hero, the true subject at the center of *The Iliad* is force," which she defines as "that X that turns anybody who is subjected to it into a thing." I may not agree with this observation of Weil's as it applies to *The Iliad*—always a dicey proposition to posit universal truths in a tale in which gods and demigods mix it up with mortals. I certainly wouldn't characterize such a force, in any event, as a "true hero." But her insight *is* applicable to ancient Athens itself. Long before Immanuel Kant's famous categorical moral imperative that we should never treat people as a means only, but as ends in themselves, Athenian Greeks practiced this in a widespread way— only then to swing in quantum fashion to the other extreme. Everyday citizens became mere means to serve the ends of a privileged and powerful few. Here Weil's insights about "force employed by man, force that enslaves man, force before which man's flesh shrinks away" are spot on. Socrates, for one, wouldn't go along and get along when this unfolded. Almost an island of *arete* unto himself, the pervasive civic cowardice surrounding him ensured that he'd be sentenced to death. Most everyone looked the other way or remained silent to the abominable act that was directed against him. Athens didn't decline gradually; it happened in the blink of an eye, when its people weren't willing to stand up for those trying to keep the door from slamming on an open society and do their part to shove it back open.

Surely the warring Athenians and Spartans were schooled in Homer's *Iliad*. Part of its timeless brilliance is that the warring Achaean Greeks and Trojans were depicted as flesh-and-blood humans in which both sides were accorded their fair share of dignity, nobility, along with hubris, arrogance, extreme brutality, as well as touching gentleness and fragility. Each believed themselves to have right and might on their side and theirs only, just as with the real-life fifth-century BC Athenians and Spartans—and, as Homer conveyed, they did, and didn't.

The epic poet also knew a thing or two about physical walls, how they could prop up the opposing sides' vainglorious images of themselves. The gods that supported each side in the war served the same purpose as the physical walls Troy had built—and as a consequence, for the longest while, they kept the Greeks' and Trojans' respective enemies at bay. Yet no matter how durable, and even when blessed with the protection of the most powerful among the pantheon of gods, the greatest physical walls sooner or later come tumbling down (and when there is something of a real-life exception, like here in Nisyros, its ancient walls still standing, they have lost their capacity to protect). In the end, Troy was sacked, its walls razed, what with Apollo and Poseidon "leading against it the force of rivers" for nine full days.

Hector, a prince and Troy's greatest fighter, had read too many of his own press clippings; he overestimated his prowess and met with an ignominious death at the hands of Achilles. Likewise, in the real world, Socrates's intimate partner Alcibiades was done in by excessive pride and conceit, try as the old philosopher might to talk some sense into him. During one of his tête-à-têtes with Alcibiades, the young scion of a wealthy family makes plain to Socrates his unbridled political ambitions. Socrates's reply (really an admonition) is this: "It is not walls or warships or arsenals that cities need, Alcibiades, if they are to be joyful," no more than it is "numbers, nor size" that make a city great. "If you are to manage the city's affairs properly and honorably," Socrates goes on to instruct Alcibiades, "you must impart *arete* to the citizens."

Arete. Excellence tinged with social conscience, with duty to self and others interlaced, each driving the other. Alcibiades, master dissembler, gave the appearance that he had taken to heart Socrates's wise words and would strive from then on to attain *arete* and become an inspiring example for his citizenry to join him in the quest. He would even go on to lead Athenians to military victory. But when the tides of war shifted to favor his opponents, he switched sides without the slightest pang of conscience or misgiving. Alcibiades pushed Athens over the cliff to its ruin. Later, he was murdered by the very Spartans he'd helped become victorious; they realized his only loyalty was to himself, and that he could just as easily betray them as he did his own people. Many scholars consider Alcibiades the West's earliest full-blown psychopath. To wreak the havoc he did, Alcibiades needed a lot of enablers and cofacilitators. One shameful way they did so was to look the other way. The other way was to look on and keep their mouths shut. The wall of craven silence erected by those who joined Alcibiades and company, as innocent people were persecuted, hounded, and worse, is a pattern and practice that has been emulated in every historical instance in which open societies (consider the Weimar Republic in Germany) close up, and quickly.

WALL THAT WON'T FALL

How is it possible that this little island of my forebears merited the construction of such formidable walls before Greece's golden age and the eventual decline of the confederation of the city-states led by Athens? Its walls outrival in quality, design, size, and durability those of far vaster and (ostensibly) more strategic populaces throughout Greece back then. What was it about this small enclave, with a currently hibernating but by no means extinct volcano, that made it so desired and tactically important all those centuries ago, and all the centuries since? How has it been shaped by conflict, and how has it shaped the outcomes of conflict?

Incredibly, Homer himself, in his eighth-century BC epic poem *The Iliad*, makes mention of Nisyros, though it's among the tiniest of the six thousand islands that are part of Greece. That he did so was almost as if to presage its centrality in terms of what would take place down the road on the island in real time and space. In his epic, the oldest extant work of Greek literature, Nisyrians both contributed and manned some of the thirty ships in the expedition against Troy that was led by the sons of King Thessalos.

Fast-forward several centuries from that fictional account: this tiny island has found itself front and center in the central conflicts of world history over the ages, starting even before the pivotal Peloponnesian War, and ever since.

How is this possible?

The ancient Greek historian Herodotus passes down to us that Nisyros's inhabitants were originally from Epidauros in the Peloponnese peninsula in southern Greece. They arrived in the early fifth century BC and promptly created a temple to worship Poseidon (and fittingly so, since it was his act that is said to have created Nisyros in the first place). The island was ruled by Artemisia I, queen of the city-state of Halicarnassus, an ally of Persia. This marked the beginning of a dizzying history over the centuries in which Nisyros's ownership caromed from one power to another that craved it for one reason or another, from its strategic locale to its bounty of resources to its astonishing natural beauty.

Even at the outset of their history, Nisyrians displayed a penchant for displaying loyalty first and foremost to themselves—a practice that continued over the centuries, for purposes principally of self-preservation. When the queen of Halicarnassus dispatched five ships filled with troops from the island to aid Persia, the Nisyrian contingent wound up deserting, and threw its support to Persia's Greek antagonists when it was clear victory would be theirs. So began not so much a checkered history but one with a "Nisyrians first" ethos.

Later that century, Nisyrians allied themselves with the first-ever confederation of Greek city-states. In effect, Nisyros was enjoying its first taste of independence, as an autonomous city-state. Even so, both to placate its larger rivals and to keep them at bay, it became a tributary to the most powerful polis of them all, Athens. When Athens launched the Peloponnesian War, Nisyrians made the calculated decision to cast their lot with the Athenians. Here again, though, in keeping with their paramount rule of safeguarding themselves first and foremost, when the winds of war shifted against Athens, they changed allegiances, just like that, and supported Sparta.

In AD 334, none other than Alexander the Great claimed supremacy over Nisyros. The island struck his fancy, along with the others in the archipelago, and he added them to his sweeping Macedonian empire. Then, in 200 BC, Nisyros allied with a number of Greek regional states to defeat its ironfisted rule—only to be sacked again, and again, and taken possession of by one autocratic ruler after another: Antony and Cleopatra (reputedly). Emperor Vespasian. The Byzantine governor of the island of Rhodes during the Fourth Crusade. Genoese forces. The Byzantine Emperor Palaiologos. The audacious Christian sect, the Knights of the Order of St. Johns on the island of Rhodes, the largest of the Dodecanese chain. The list of its possessors goes on like a Who's Who of despots and tyrants.

In 1455, after the fall of Constantinople by the invading Ottomans, they dispatched a fleet to claim Nisyros. Much of the island's populace was either wiped out by the sweeping annihilation campaign of Sultan Mehmet II, or was enslaved and sold elsewhere like so much chattel. Nisyros *did* eventually return to the dominion of the rulers of Rhodes, and then of Catalan, but only for it then to be retaken—not once, but twice—by the ruthless Ottomans. It wasn't until the latter half of the eighteenth century that Nisyrians could take a breather from their merciless straits under the tyranny of the Ottomans, after their conquerors had to divert their focus and expend their military resources in the thirteen-year Russo-Turkish War that didn't conclude until 1792. Nisyrians took advantage of this lull to support the Greek Revolution of 1821, providing troops to help man the fleet of the renowned Greek admiral, Andreas Miaoulis. As its reward, Nisyros experienced another fleeting taste of freedom; in 1823, it accepted the invitation to join the Provisional Administration of Free Greece. Shortly afterward, Nisyros yet again was conquered by the Ottomans and again had to submit to their rule.

At long last, in 1912, Turkish rule of Nisyros ended once and for all when it and the other Dodecanese islands were seized by an Italian war fleet that already had annexed North African territories once controlled by Turkey. Though welcomed at first as liberators, the Italians soon transformed the islands into permanent colonies. In 1923, just as my grandparents were set to escape Nisyros for the second time, the Treaty of Lausanne was signed. It stipulated that Turkey permanently cede the islands to the Italian fascists. Native resentment toward the Italians grew with the introduction of harsh taxation measures, the nationalization of Greek businesses, and in 1937, its disparaging move to relegate the island's Greek language to the status of a mere regional tongue.

Following Italy's surrender to the Allies in 1943, the Dodecanese passed into German hands. Nisyrians this time had had enough of subjugation; they zealously resisted the new occupiers. On May 8, 1945, Germany surrendered the Dodecanese to the Allied forces. After that momentous occasion, Nisyros was placed under British protection. Then, on March 31, 1947, the island and its overwhelmingly ethnic Greek population was made an official part of Greece, and has been so ever since.

By this time, twenty-four years had passed since my grandparents once and for all had left behind their immediate and extended family on the island.

ISLAND PRISON

My grandparents—Philip Dimitrios Philipou, my namesake, and his wife, my *yaya*, Calliope Kavazarakis Philipou—crossed the threshold of what they and more than twelve million others considered the promised land of the United States through Ellis Island. For them, Nisyros had been a prison. It offered no possibility of escape from poverty. Better by far to risk it all in the U.S. My grandparents' Ellis Island entry documents, preserved by the Immigration and Naturalization Service, classify them as ethnic Greeks and Italian citizens. The first time they set foot on U.S. soil, on March 29, 1910, they arrived on the SS *Chicago*. Just a year earlier, during the Italo-Turkish war, Nisyros had passed from longtime Ottoman and Turkish rule to the dominion of what was then the Kingdom of Italy. For Nisyrians like Philip and Calliope, who were from society's lower rungs, the change created even more instability and less economic opportunity. Even though my *yaya* was the oldest of all her six brothers and sisters, and as such in that matrilineal society, she stood to inherit all the family properties, at the time they were worth next to nothing.

The second time around, when my grandparents again made the trip from Nisyros to the U.S., this time arriving on January 10, 1923, they crossed the Atlantic Ocean on the SS *Acropolis*. By then, the island was under the grip of Prime Minister Benito Mussolini and his National Fascist Party. Nisyros was coveted for its strategic location as a launching pad for expanding their envisioned empire. Philip and Calliope left in the nick of time. If they'd at-

tempted to depart even a few months later, Mussolini and his min-
ions would have waylaid them. Even if they'd managed to somehow escape later on, a double whammy would have awaited them
on the other side of the ocean, since by then, a nativist majority in
the U.S. Congress had enacted a draconian law prohibiting the
entry of any further "southern Greeks and Italians"—read: the
poorest European immigrants.

Why were they in this near-perilous predicament in the first
place? How is it possible that they'd made the harrowing journey
from Nisyros to the U.S., only to do a double take and repeat that
same journey? It just wasn't done. Yet they did just that.

One might reasonably surmise that perhaps they didn't mind
such voyages, even though they required travel for six weeks across
the Atlantic in the cramped and unsanitary conditions of those who
bought the cheapest steerage tickets for $30 apiece—still a princely
sum for them—from agents who sold them from island to island.
After all, they came from families of voyagers, boatmen, and sea-
farers. But no, that's not why. My *yaya* returned to the island in
1922 without telling her husband. She is said to have had a lover. A
distraught Philip scrimped and saved to make the ocean trek back
himself some months later. He was dead set on convincing his wife
to rejoin him in the U.S. After his beseeching entreaties, Yaya gave
in, albeit with a heavy heart.

My grandfather, his heart broken but madly in love with my
handsome but not pretty *yaya*—she had a certain air, a certain je ne
sais quoi, that allured men of intelligence and wit (but not fortune)—won the day. He coaxed her into giving the U.S. (and him)
another chance. Their journey back this time was on the SS *Acropolis*. They arrived at Ellis Island on January 10, 1923. Unlike the
first time, in which their entry was smooth sailing, this time there
was a hitch. During this latest round of processing, Philip became a
"detained petitioner." He was put in a cell on the south side of the
island while an investigation ensued into alleged acts on his part

while in Nisyros. Rumor, never confirmed, had it that he had a serious altercation (or worse) with a Nisyrian of Greek Turkish descent who—again, rumor had it—had been cavorting with his wife.

Philip received in his cramped detention cell a letter dated January 26, 1923, from two of his brothers in New York City. They assured him that they were exhausting every avenue to get him released. They relayed that they were in the throes of making earnest appeals directly to New York's then mayor, J. Peter Grace, and to their congressman in Washington, D.C. Meanwhile, they assured Philip, if they had anything to do with it, he'd "be out from jail in a few days." In the interim, they were sending him "two nice cigars" in order to "forget your troubles" for a while.

Their efforts paid off. My grandfather was released soon afterward. Several months later, my uncle Dimitrios, or Jimmy, was born. Dad shared with me that his older brother bore over the years the brunt of their father Philip's infrequent but petrifying bursts of anger. Dad told me that once when he was about six years old, during an argument Philip was having with their mother, his brave brother tried to step in between them. Philip whipped around, grabbed his light and lithe sixteen-year-old son Jimmy, lifted him over the balcony, and held him dangling over the edge by the ankles. Dad said that only the plaintive screams of their mother, which attracted the attention of neighbors, and might have brought the police, got him to pull Uncle Jimmy back to safe ground. The spring before he died, Dad told me the reason for his father's misplaced anger toward his older brother, who did not resemble him or his sister or his father.

WALL OF SPIRITS

I know I will never see my dad again.

I see my dad everywhere.

The last time I saw Dad alive, he had invited my family to spend a glorious week with him at a Florida resort. Over the course of many late-night confabs, he shared with me some eye-opening things about others in his orbit, one in particular. The look of hurt and betrayal on his face as he did so was hard to countenance. It was rare for Dad ever to wear his emotions on his sleeve. He had borne with grace and dignity, perseverance and even buoyancy more than his fair share of hardships since his childhood, including the death of his own father when he was at a tender age, making it necessary for him to be a breadwinner of the family. Dad never was one to wallow in pity or to be mired in resentment. But he was only human, and he reached his tipping point in his seventy-eighth year; he shared with me that he'd been played for a patsy. Though love, devotion, and innocence itself can be kinds of virtues in certain contexts, they can be seen as pathetic and even laughable weaknesses by those with malintent who would exploit such vulnerabilities without the slightest remorse. I love and admire Dad—as shrewd and savvy as they come in so many regards—all the more for his innocence in this instance. Just as I have lasting regret that, like my dad, I had not begun to remotely fathom who and what he was contending with.

By the time caring others arrived at my dad's condominium after learning of his death, most of its contents had been removed. My father was the ultimate pack rat, yet his home was nearly cleaned out. Gone were all the signed books of mine that I'd given him over the years, as well as mountains of family memorabilia, including his extensive collection of home movies that he himself had made over the course of nearly sixty years. Gone was his abundant coin collection that he'd been building since a child selling newspapers on Tampa street corners (I have a photocopy of the original 1945 article, from the *Tampa Times*, that was removed from his home about "young Alex Phillips (he is 12) . . . in a downtown restaurant selling the *Night Final* when a young lady . . . gave Alex a 1913 quarter," the thirty-two-year-old coin already worth a considerable amount—and so began his lifelong coin-collecting passion). Gone also were nearly all his financial statements, bonds, stock certificates, and cash, including what he called his "personal ATM" of several thousand dollars that he always kept in a suit pocket in his closet. Even a birthday card he'd bought for my oldest daughter had been put through a shredder.

By the time I myself arrived at Dad's home, it was largely devoid of the many belongings that reflected his rich and colorful history and personality, his eclectic tastes in art and music, his wide cultural interests, even if the most special place in his heart was reserved for those of Greek origin or influence. I went from room to room in his unrecognizably neat home in an aimless, abstracted way. Only a handful of Dad's many books remained on the premises, along with a few pieces of furniture, and some carefully stacked items on his dining room hutch that was normally strewn with precarious piles of documents. It likely would have taken at least a week of almost nonstop effort to have emptied the bulk of his belongings from his home (yet apparently, according to the first close companion of Dad's who arrived at his condominium after learning of his death, no one previously on hand had bothered to clean the sheets on which he'd soiled himself shortly before he died; disgusted, she washed them herself).

At Dad's office desk, a few books lay on the top. Clearly they were considered of no value by whoever had rifled through everything and removed most of his other possessions. Two of them were weather-beaten books that had belonged to Uncle Jimmy, who'd read passages from them to me shortly before he died in 2001. I brought the two volumes to the sofa in the family room. Dad had told me once, years ago, that he had put them away for safekeeping.

Each volume had a bookmark extending out of it. They were identical leather bookmarks that I believe were from my uncle Jimmy's days at the University of Tampa. I opened the Shakespeare collection to the bookmarked page. An underlined passage in *Henry V*, act 4, scene 1 of the play was one my uncle had once read to me. I read the words of King Henry aloud: "There is some soul of goodness in things evil, would men observingly distill it out. For our bad neighbors make us early stirrers, which is both healthful and good husbandry; besides, they are outward consciences, and preachers to us all, admonishing that we should dress us fairly."

Could it be that these books weren't left haphazardly? Could this be some sort of admonition and admission at one and the same time by whoever left it here? Are bad friends and family and neighbors (among others) reminders of who we ourselves might have turned out to be—and might still, depending? Are they our outward consciences, mirrors into the dark parts of our own hearts? Do they make those of us who are of fairly healthful and good husbandry realize "there but for the grace of God go I"? Can it be that true goodness of soul is to realize the folly of constructing chimeric walls between those deemed good and those deemed evil?

Then I opened the bookmark in the volume of Shelley's works. Underlined were parts of *Prometheus Unbound*: "To suffer woes which Hope thinks infinite; to forgive wrongs darker than death or night . . . to love, and bear; to hope till Hope creates from its own wreck the thing it contemplates. Neither to change nor falter nor repent; This . . . is to be Good, great and joyous, beautiful and free."

As many times as I've pondered these words since the occasion, well over a decade earlier, my uncle had read them to me, they sink in now more than ever. How do you forgive wrongs that are darker than night or death? Is forgiveness beside the point? Are loving and bearing, born of deeper understanding and even empathy, what matter most, more than ever?

Even though the events surrounding Dad's death could have unfolded in myriad other ways, this is how they did unfold. How can I accept this, without resignation, and without faltering regret?

How can I grow from this, in ways that might resonate with others far and wide? In what ways can I best hold on to my beloved late father for dear life, and in what others might I best let go of him for dear life, if my quest for self-knowledge and human *arete* is to continue on an upward trajectory?

I sat on the sofa, those books on my lap, unaware of the passage of time. At some point, I felt a small lump inside the inside leaf of one book jacket. A thick, square piece of paper fell out. It had to be unfolded again and again before it was fully open. It was a poem, "6,051." It was written in my *yaya*'s unmistakable script. The poem was one that Uncle Jimmy had told me she once had written that he had discovered hidden in her jewelry box, and that he'd said he'd discarded. He must have appropriated it as a boy and never breathed a word of it to anyone. No one could keep a secret like my dad and his brother. No one. I think the only two people they ever fully trusted were one another.

Now here I am in Nisyros, at the other end of all those 6,051 miles.

WALL OF VISION

I pull out my binoculars for the first time and look out from the acropolis wall at the many fishing boats in the distance. Boats of sundry sizes and colors—some moored, some on their way out to deeper waters, some on their way back in, some with full catches, some with sparse ones. With his stellar professional success in a key role—overseeing the construction of the U.S. Navy's nuclear aircraft carrier fleet—Dad had brought his family of watermen and waterwomen full circle, and to loftier heights than they could have ever conceived of.

Just then, Calliope—the name of Greek mythology's oldest muse, of wisdom and poetry, and the namesake and great-great-grandniece of my *yaya*—arrives on the scene. My second cousin is accompanied by her great-grandfather Matthias. They make their way up the wall's wide interior stone steps to where I'm sitting. Matthias, spry as a mountain goat, hasn't so much as broken a sweat after the long, uneven, and at times steep climb from his village. He is now 102, not an unusual age among Greeks on the islands; they often attribute it to their pescatarian diet, which I long ago adopted (though unlike me, many of them, including Matthias, drink socially and smoke the occasional cigar or cigarette).

Matthias had known my uncle Jimmy. Like my uncle, he had fought in World War II, in his case as a Greek soldier who was part of the Allied forces. He'd fought valiantly, with limitless contempt and hatred for Mussolini, who was responsible for the imprisonment and death by hanging of friends and relatives who'd taken a stand against him. Matthias was three years old when my grandparents emigrated in 1923. His own father had been close to my grandfather Philip, as well as to my *yaya*.

Calliope, or Popi for short, was born and raised in New York, where her great-grandfather George—my grandfather Philip's brother and the one who helped get him released from detention—settled in 1915, some years before my father's parents came to the U.S. Calliope is a sought-after architect, with clients in New York, Athens, and Nisyros. Her great-grandfather had been a successful businessman and beloved philanthropist. I never met him in person, but I vividly remember George, a mover and shaker in the Nisyrian Society of New York, for the wonderful Christmas gifts he sent me, including my very first record player, and for our long phone conversations each and every Christmas Day.

Calliope and Matthias sit to my left. Matthias, who had been a public school literature teacher for over half a century, points to the space to my right. "Your father was right there," he says matter-of-factly. Does he see spirits too? I give him a quizzical look with a raised eyebrow. He says no more.

Soon after I arrived in Nisyros, I'd poured out much of my heart, particularly to Calliope. It hadn't been my intention to do so, but Calliope sees inside and through me like few others. She and Matthias sit in silence with me now. Calliope looks out at the vast expanse of sea. It is a sight you can never weary of. Matthias hasn't taken his eyes off me. "Don't despise the person at the center of this," he says in Greek in due time. "Such people despise themselves far more than any of us ever could. Nothing, and no amount of money, will compensate for that.

"You know, we're all proud of you, Christóforos"—my full middle name in Greek—"all you've done to promote and practice the best of your heritage," Matthias says next. "No one more than your father. When Alexandros was here, he sat right there beside where you're sitting now." He again points with a gnarled forefinger to the empty space on the other side of me. "You've never seen or heard a father prouder of a son."

At first, the words don't sink in. "My father . . . was here?"

Matthias's reply is evasive. "He could be very secretive, your father. That's how you survive when you have to fend for yourself starting so young."

Eventually, he says, "Some things you can never imagine people capable of doing, because if you do imagine it, you may feel it reflects back on you."

Calliope, a decade my junior, has not said a word up until now. I came to Nisyros at this point in time—the coronavirus pandemic looming, unbeknownst to me—in part because I knew she was here. When I was in the throes of establishing my first ongoing Socrates Café, in Montclair, New Jersey, in 1996—it still convenes each week after all these years—she and I met up a number of times in New York. We hit it off at once, two overachieving cousins from humble backgrounds determined to live creative lives and push ourselves to the limit. Calliope also somehow found time, and had the talent, to be cast in several Off-Broadway shows while also a rising star architect. We'd lose track of time chatting across from one another at café tables as only two long-lost cousins and soul-mates who at last have found one another can.

Agate-eyed Calliope, bright and shining and effervescent, has had one flame-and-burn personal relationship after another over the years, the promise of subliminal eros turned to heartache. Yet I've never met anyone more in love with life itself. She had known my uncle Jimmy well, and like him and me both, she has an abiding love of poetry. Also like him and me, she dabbles in composing it herself on occasion.

Now Calliope, her face turned away from me and Matthias, says to no one in particular, her melodic voice at a volume that makes it seem to come from the wind itself swirling around us: "To suffer woes which hope thinks infinite; to forgive wrongs darker than death or night . . . to love, and bear; to hope till hope creates from its own wreck the thing it contemplates. . . . Neither to change, nor falter, nor repent. This . . . is to be Good, great and joyous, beautiful and free."

I had mentioned earlier these verses to her and Matthias, along with the Shakespeare passage from *Henry V*, and how they'd been in the few books left in my father's home after he died. Calliope tells me now, "Dimitrios, Uncle Jimmy, told me you two had talked from dusk until dawn one night. He'd shared those passages with me, too. I read them again when, ten days after his death, our dear cousin was killed in the World Trade Center attacks."

On September 11, 2001, one of our cousins, an investment advisor working on the 104th floor of the North Tower, was killed. Part of Calliope's impassioned and compassionate response to the horrific events of that day was to become part of an effort to provide vital outreach and assistance to families who'd lost loved ones that day. As she told me when she first threw herself heart and soul into this effort, "The best way to respond to acts of hate is to become a better person yourself."

Since then, she has taken on other noble causes. Indeed, Calliope and I were able to rendezvous in Nisyros primarily because she hadn't been far away—on the Greece-Turkey border to help set up mobile libraries in refugee camps for asylum seekers—from Syria, Afghanistan, Pakistan, Iraq, Iran—this at a time when Greek officials are taking a hard-line stance against their attempts to cross into their country for safe sanctuary. Calliope felt the dislocated people's pain. My cousin channels her own setbacks and sufferings into acts toward others of enduring love and goodness. Anyone blessed to be part of her orbit can't help but want to become a better person.

Eventually Matthias says, "You had to come here, Christóforos. This is your Delphi."

"*One* of your Delphis," Calliope corrects. "Socrates claimed to be a citizen of the world. You really are, Christóforos. The path you've chosen isn't for the faint of heart. You can't stop taking it now. If you do stop, those who commit evil win."

How do you continue on the path when your soul is crushed, heart shattered? How do you go on when the truth might be that all your work "seeking Socrates" to tear down walls and build bridges of love and understanding between even the most different and differing human beings has been for naught? When you were so busy trying to save the world that you couldn't save your own father?

The only person who can read my mind and heart with hardly a word uttered by yours truly, besides my wife, is Calliope. I say plaintively, "How?"

"'There is some soul of goodness in things evil, would men observingly distill it out,'" my cousin and grandmother's wise namesake says. "You're a seeker, Christóforos. You have a heretic's heart. You've shown the same love for and understanding of inmates at maximum security prisons as you have the most prominent and well regarded. You've shown that they can have virtuous and altruistic sides, and sometimes more than the most prominent and well-regarded.

"Maybe there's a reason or explanation why you, of all people, have to endure something like this. I don't know. I *do* know that if there *are* answers for how to forgive wrongs darker than death or night, how to love, bear, and hope, then they lie in the kind of seeking that you've dedicated your life to."

NOTE

1. Socrates was by no means alone in this; the likes of Plato and even Aristotle, "Mr. Rationality" himself, also accepted at face value the pronouncements of the succession of oracle priestesses there. It's also well worth noting that in Socrates's other unforgettable interaction with a woman—the seer and priestess Diotima of Mantinea in the *Symposium*—he deferred to her as well; he listens with full absorption in a way that he never did with his male interlocutors. Socrates goes so far as to say—again with uncharacteristic humility—that everything he learned about love matters is thanks to her.

Part I

In-Between Worlds

As I leave Nisyros, my heart is heavier the greater the distance grows from the land of my forebears. I crave more intimate give-and-takes of the kind I had with my cousin. I think of my *yaya*, as well as of Xenophon, a friend and contemporary of Socrates.

On the day I became a teenager, my *yaya* gifted me another book—just months, it would turn out, before she died at age seventy-seven. "You're coming of age present," she said. It was a collection of the historian Xenophon's conversations with Socrates. The two had long reveled in one another's company, and held numerous one-on-one exchanges over the course of the years.

Xenophon's contributions to our insights on Socrates have long played second fiddle to Plato's Socratic oeuvre—and to our detriment. The fact that Xenophon himself is not considered a philosopher per se, as Socrates's other scribe Plato was, surely has much to do with it, relegating his writings regarding the most famed philosopher of old to the shadows. Yet in their way, his writings are equally valuable. We gain greater understanding of Socrates himself, and of another important way he went about communing with others.

Virtually all of Plato's Socratic dialogues feature the "chorale" approach to the Greek philosopher's inquiries—and little wonder a dramatist like Plato would prefer an array of interlocutors philosophizing with Socrates in a methodical manner, building up to a crescendo. In counterpoint, Xenophon passes down to us a Socrates—as much a mentor to him as to Plato—who is comfortable with one-on-one discourses. Xenophon presents to us a Socrates who locks hearts and minds in closer, more confidential tête-à-têtes, usually with one person at a time. What's more, these exchanges often are far more prescriptive than Plato's. Concrete suggestions and advice are routinely proffered by Socrates and his fellow conversers. Though not discursive inquiries of the kind Plato depicts Socrates partaking in, they nonetheless put on prominent display a great mind and heart at work and in order to learn how better to become a practitioner of excellence in all life's dimensions.

Take Xenophon's "The Dinner Party," a brilliant rendering of Socrates engaging in a number of one-on-one dialogues over the course of the soiree. It is a fascinating blend of, and oscillation between, idle and not so idle chitchat on the nature of love, admixed with tête-à-tête confabs of a philosophical kind that Socrates had with some seated around him. The intriguing questions discussed: What are you most proud of when it comes to your works and deeds? Should you love yourself or another first and foremost for one's mind or for one's physical features and attractions?

As Xenophon shows us, Socrates is, as always, seeking—but in this case in a far more up close and personal, accessible, and everyday way. While more rambling and prone to tangents than Plato's queries that feature Socrates front and center, they are often in their own right piercing. All told, they provide a more fleshed-out measure of our foremost Western philosopher. They show his more human side—less ironic, less close to the vest when it comes to sharing his own normative views and prescriptions, more open to others.

Alas, even someone normally as perspicacious as the British philosopher and polymath Bertrand Russell shows his snootiness toward Xenophon; Russell characterizes him as "not very liberally endowed with brains, and on the whole conventional in his outlook." Even the likes of Russell fails to appreciate that Xenophon makes us privy to a more conventional, less forbidding or offputting side of Socrates—no less profound, in my estimation, and as wickedly rational as ever.

Xenophon further limns a more introspective Socrates who first and foremost is engaged in self-examination, or really, self-revelation. Understanding this side of him gives one fresher eyes when poring over Plato's dialogues in which Socrates figures most prominently; they render him more accessible and relatable. Plato chose to shape his observations of Socrates in action around the famed philosopher's public inquiries among groups, while Xenophon shows us a side of him engaged in far more intimate banter. One of Plato's ultimate aims is to shed light in a more ethereal way on what it means to Socrates to have "healthiness of soul." Xenophon's, on the other hand, is to spotlight how the more down-to-earth Socrates shows what human goodness can amount to. Both have their eyes on the same prize, even as they are intent on sharing singularly different dimensions of the seventy-something philosopher in darkening times.

In my own practice with Socrates Café, I have largely emulated the Socrates who takes a more collective approach to teasing out truths. Yet it dawns on me now, on the plane trip back to Athens—where I'll catch the first of three connecting flights to my next destination in the southernmost part of North America—that Socrates's one-on-one discourses that Xenophon shares with us are pregnant with meaning in their own right. This version of Socrates traverses the space between the formal and informal, the conversational and explorational, the public and the private, the intentional and serendipitous.

I ask myself: What if, in my more confidential encounters, I make a conscious and conscientious effort to tap into this neglected, more conversational side of the Socratic tradition of understanding and insight? After my intensive back-and-forths with my cousin and great-uncle in Nisyros, I'm convinced unique answers lie in this kind of seeking—answers not just for my particular plight, but that might be applicable to others struggling to deal with unfathomable loss or betrayal (a kind of loss), and more positively, to discover renewed love, forbearance, and hope at the other end of a tunnel that seems darker than death or night.

BEYOND GOOD AND EVIL

My perch on the acropolis wall of Nisyros is now one of my Delphis, a place that affords me an inside-out and outside-in mirror into my inmost self. From Nisyros, I then journey more than eleven thousand kilometers (over seven thousand miles) to another destination that has long been for me a kind of Delphi.

Now I am ascending hundreds of steep steps to a centuries-old *templo* in San Cristobal de las Casas in Chiapas, Mexico. The nonprofit organization Democracy Café, which I founded and still oversee, is in the throes of launching in this region a program for children who are victims of familial abuse and living in shelters. I will be giving the following day a facilitators training workshop to volunteers who will implement the program here. I take advantage of my free day today to seek out Veruch in the central plaza or *zocalo* of this colonial city in the Chiapas highlands where I once lived.

She is walking in lockstep with me now. I haven't seen her in a decade. She is taller than me now, her bright eyes brimming and dancing with pleasure that we have reunited at long last. I first met Veruch, her name in the Mayan dialect of Tzotzil, soon after my wife, Ceci, and I made San Cristobal de las Casas our home for a full decade starting in 2000. Over the ensuing years, Veruch, her mother Maruch, and little brother Mario became close friends of ours. Ceci had been a teacher in an indigenous community in Chiapas before she and I met and fell in love—at a Socrates Café, in New Jersey no less, shortly after she'd arrived there to earn her master's degree, and when she was the only person to attend.

Nestled in the highlands among deep green, cloud-capped hills, the once-insular city of San Cristobal de las Casas itself, founded in 1527 and situated 2,113 meters (6,932 feet) in the air, is a multicultural and multiethnic mecca. It is also home to several centuries-old *templos*, each with a distinct architectural design, some dating back as far as to the sixteenth century.

At the lookouts, or *miradores*, surrounding this particular temple atop the *cerrito*, or little hill, that Veruch and I ascend, we're treated to a glorious panoramic view of the centuries-old city, the surrounding hillsides and valleys, and the many communities that populate its outskirts, including vast outposts of families of a number of distinct indigenous groups, including Maya, Tzotzils, Tzeltals, and Lacondons. They have settled on property not technically theirs after they were ejected from their traditional communities, or *ediles*, because of political and religious differences with the principal power brokers.

The rich mosaic of artistry and artisanship, customs and ethnicities, traditions and practices in San Cristobal that coalesce here also now often clash these days, driven in part by ever-growing socioeconomic disparities between the haves and have-nots. The rising tensions, also triggered by racism and classism and the political differences that spring from them, are sometimes palpable. Questions pertaining to issues of fundamental rights of the many indigenous groups that live in this region have never been resolved, and as a consequence, simmering tensions are again a ticking time bomb that first came to a head in real violence during the Zapatista uprising in Chiapas launched in 1994. In the years since, the EZLN

(Zapatista Army of National Liberation) has remained a formidable presence, even as its influence has waned and waxed. The issues for which it has engaged in struggle via both violent and nonviolent strategies remain unresolved.

What is most striking during the drive to San Cristobal de las Casas from the airport is the massive deforestation of the surrounding area, and along with it the eerie disappearance of local flora and fauna, that now mars the scenery—and accompanying this, the radical change in climate. The traditional cool and rainy season that started in April and ended sometime in November is now sporadic at best, with heavy rain maybe one day every week or two, rather than daily and beginning like clockwork at midday.

It is in this vexing context that I return to San Cristobal de las Casas and, after all these years, find Veruch where she habitually had been when I lived there, and still is, at this day and hour—in the city's main historic plaza. A tourist is examining her handwoven goods draped over her arms when she sees me and runs over. Not normally one for effusive displays, she gives me a bear hug.

Soon after, Veruch and I make our way up the "little" hill. At the cerrito's summit, near the edge of a steep cliff, is perched the temple, looking almost as if it is sprung from the earth itself. Diminutive yet eye catching, called *Templo El Cerrito* or *Templo San Cristobalito*, the church is actually on high elevation. As Veruch and I continue the climb upward, I think about the first time I serendipitously encountered her when she was twelve years old. That day, I stood in the plaza made of limestone and took in the surrounding view. This is one of those places, almost mystical, where you can't help but feel closer both to the immensity and to yourself. To my unbelieving ears, I heard piano music inside the little church—and music, at that, that was the furthest thing from any you'd expect to emanate from inside a house of worship. Someone was playing Beethoven's "Ode to Joy" with a toe-tapping abandon that a Beethoven purist would find cringeworthy, but that I suspect would have delighted the composer himself.

I made a beeline for the entrance of the *templo*. I passed through the entrance of its simple, elegant façade, even though a sign said it was closed to the public for the moment. There in semidarkness—circlets of light wafting through stained glass windows, projecting onto the wooden floor like little spotlights—sat a wisp of a child. She was in indigenous garb—a bright blue *huipil* or blouse, a wool *enredo* or tube skirt dyed in indigo and gray, and a bright white woven cotton sash—hunched over a piano, over which a sign says, "Do not play/*favor de no tocar*."

When she was done, I clapped and said, "Wow" in Spanish (*guau*). I startled her. She walked quickly past me, her rubber sandals, or *chanclas*, gliding across the floor. She retrieved from the floor her bundle of multicolored handwoven belts (*cinturones*), shawls (*chales*), scarves (*bufondas*), necklaces (*pendientes*), bracelets (*pulseras*), and baby carriers (*rebozos*). My wife and I had bought many such goods from indigenous families, particularly from the children who sold them in San Cristobal's principal historical plaza (which now is blemished with signs for a multinational soft drink company). Even at quick glance, it was evident that these items were made with inordinate artistry.

She was about to beat a hasty retreat when I told her I wanted to buy some of her goods. My purchases included a *rebozo* to tote our soon-to-be baby girl. Veruch told me that ever since she could stand up, she toiled seven days a week, asking tourists and locals to buy her goods, all of which she and her mother make themselves. Becoming a piano player had added a new dimension to her life, she then shared. Veruch told me she'd learned to play when her older sister, Loxa (pronounced Lo-*sha*), was herself learning. The instructor was Loxa's lover, an American, and a pianist. She told me Loxa and Eric were now in the U.S., Loxa now among its millions of undocumented. Eric had paid for Loxa to be spirited into the country by a *coyote* who transported undocumented people across the Sonoran Desert—people who were determined to enter the U.S. for much the same reason my grandparents did. Veruch said that her sister and lover left one night without so much as a goodbye. She said they departed without their baby, leaving her and her mother to care for little Andreas in the small shanty of corrugated aluminum with a dirt floor in which they lived. Ever since then, during siesta hour, when sales in the main plaza came to a standstill, Veruch made the ascent to the church, where she'd been given permission to play the piano. Often her brother Mario and their baby nephew Andreas came with her.

Veruch told me, that first day we met, that her own father had been killed in a drunken brawl years before. I asked her how. "*Bala*" was her reply. Bullet. It is a too common story. Veruch's mother raised her and her brother Mario, and now was also bringing up her grandson Andreas whom Eric and Loxa had left behind. But in truth, Veruch and Mario also supported and even raised one another; Veruch for one was just as much of a primary income earner and took care of the younger ones every bit as much as her mother, and Mario sometimes worked in the *milpa*, plots of land where traditional corn, called *maiz*, is grown, particularly during planting and harvesting season.

From that chance encounter, a friendship was born. Ceci and I often rendezvoused with her and her family, including her little brother, a good-natured boy with endless energy and (like Veruch) a sweeping curiosity about anything, and their baby nephew Andreas, his skin light and eyes a translucent gray, his nature bubbly. That baby knew he was loved. Veruch and her mother often would gather together other Tzotzils to join us in Philosophers' Club inquiries for children and youth, and Socrates Cafés for adults and children alike. Even though Mexico's indigenous have been victims of unspeakable oppression and brutality for generations on end by the endemically corrupt and racist political system in Mexico—

one that to this day refuses to recognize fully indigenous rights—
they still continue, wherever they live, the tradition of inquiring and
problem solving among themselves as full equals. Part of this circle
tradition of theirs surely is also due to the fact that they don't look
at time in a linear way—past, present, future—but instead in circular fashion, with important events taking place in what they call
"time circles," a "pattern" of time in which events are arranged
according to their level of importance for each person and his or her
community as a whole, rather than in the chronological Western
time sequence. So, for them, when convening a Socrates Café or
any other gathering of import, they "place" it in their innermost
circle of time.

At one of our philosophical gatherings, I'd proposed that we
explore the question "What is a good human being?" But Veruch
told me I wasn't asking the right question. She said we needed to
examine, "What is a true human being?" She explained to me that
Tzotzils had no conception of what a *good* human being might or
might not be—only of what a *batsil winic*, or a *true* human being,
was. She proceeded to instruct me that in the Tzotzil belief system,
you enter this world as a "mere human being." To become a *true*
human being, she went on, you have to show that you merit this
moniker.

I asked her that day—in Spanish, our bridge language—to describe to me such a person. Her reply was the last one I expected:
"A true human being is someone who, when I try to sell him or her
one of my handmade goods replies politely, 'No, thank you.'" Veruch went on to explain that far more often than not, the people of
means she encounters in the plazas walk brusquely past her without
so much as recognizing her existence, and that a number of them
intentionally elbow her aside. Some, she said, even forcefully push
her to the ground. "When they at least look me in the eyes, when
they say, maybe with smile, 'No thank you,' they're recognizing
me as a person, a fellow human being. That shows goodness, kind-

ness. They're true human beings, *batsil winic*, because they see me, too, as a human being."

What she shared brought to mind the German-born American philosopher and political theorist Hannah Arendt's powerful assertion that our entrance into this world as newborns is not what matters most when it comes to matters of personhood. While our beginning as an individual "is guaranteed by each new birth," there must be an ongoing birthing process—a "second birth," which Arendt claims can only be had through our demonstrated works and words and deeds. As she puts it in *The Human Condition*, "with word and deed we insert ourselves into the human world, and this insertion is like a second birth." Until and unless this takes place, she asserts, we are existentially stillborn, not full-fledged persons. As I write in my book *A Child at Heart*, by this conception of Arendt's (and Veruch's), those who have treated Veruch and other indigenous children—or anyone else—as less than their equal are mere human beings, because they deliberately try to deny others their place as equals at the sociopolitical table, their acts of rejection and exclusion aimed at preventing their unfolding—but in point of fact, such oppressors just as much (if not more) prevent their own unfolding.

The indigenous people I have encountered in Chiapas—in counterpoint to those who seek to subjugate—in spite of the many hardships they face every day, are consummate sharers. I have found that no matter how little they have, they distribute among others in need what little they have. If only all of us could, as they are, be more advanced along the path toward becoming a *batsil winic*, what a brighter time it would herald for one and all.

As I look at Veruch on this day that we reunite after so many years, as joyful as we both are, her brow also cannot mask that it is etched with some pain. After the ascent, we settle on a marble bench with a magnificent view. She unslings her *rebozo* from her back near the Temple of San Cristobalito and takes out a sleeping baby Mario, named after her brother. He slowly awakens to her coos. He looks at me and gurgles with what seems genuine pleasure before she begins to breastfeed him.

Veruch eventually tells me the tragic tidings: three years earlier, at age twenty, her brother Mario met with the same fate as their father, and in the same way. "I named my baby after him," she says after that. "I can tell already they look a lot alike, and will have the same personality. I will make sure my baby lives a long life."

After a while, she pulls a book from her embroidered satchel. It's a Spanish edition of my first philosophical children's book, *The Philosophers' Club*, or *Club de Los Filosofos*, that I had given to her all those years ago. (During those years in San Cristobal de las Casas, Ceci taught Veruch and Mario, among scores of other indigenous children, to read in a volunteer classroom without walls project she established.) I open the book and behold a marvel: Veruch has translated every line into her native Tzotzil, and transposed the original pages of Spanish text into text of her own tongue. She tells me she uses the book to teach other Tzotzil children to read, and that also, they cluster around her many evenings, and, after she reads one or more of the book's questions out loud, then they launch into philosophical exchanges. She sees how pleased I am, claps her hands in delight.

"My mother made me sell the phone you gave me, you see," she then says. "But she did give me enough of the proceeds to have my translation typeset and put into pretty print."

I ask Veruch about her mother. She does not offer a reply at first. After a while, she says, "Last summer, Mama went to Cozumel on the coast to sell to tourists at the beach there. I stayed behind to keep watch on our property, since some thugs of the government had been trying to remove us from it, even though we'd bought it with money we'd saved for years. Mama didn't come back. Her companions said she'd gone alone to the beach one morning, earlier than the rest. . . ."

Later, Veruch looks at me and says, "You've lost someone, too, Christopher."

I tell her some of my story. A good while later, she says, "What's something good that someone did for you who also did evil to you or to someone you love?"

I tell her about a time a German shepherd attacked me. It severely bit both of my legs, blood pouring out of the puncture wounds, and was in the process of lunging for my neck, when someone who fits her description arrived on the scene and drove off the dog at considerable personal risk.

"Tell me something your father did to someone that was evil," she says next, after a considerable pause.

"Words can be evil things when they are used to wound," she says when I'm done. "They can cut deeper than a real knife, and not only never heal, but cause ever more hurt as time passes."

Then she asks me, "What's the worst thing you've ever done?"

Before I know it, I'm telling her about an action of mine that caused great anguish to one I love dearly. "You are still *batsil winic*," she says some time afterward. "True human beings aren't perfect. But they do recognize the hurts they've caused and try their best to make amends, and never to repeat it. We're all darkness and light, Christopher. When *batsil winic* do dark things, they learn from them, so they can better serve the good and the light."

Dusk arrives. As if on cue, a bat, *un murcielago*, appears and circles directly overhead. I then realize that bats are now out and about everywhere.

"*Zotzilaha* is guardian of the Tzotzil," Veruch tells me. "He rules over the darkness, protects us from our enemies. *Zotzilaha* isn't pure good. He has equal parts darkness and light. He couldn't protect us from the powerful forces of darkness if he didn't have darkness himself and understand it, so he can wield his powerful light to keep it at bay. You never defeat darkness, but you can make sure the light wins the day."

Centuries ago, the Tzotzil indigenous—or Zotzil Maya as they were originally called—of which Veruch and her family are part, called themselves *Zotzil winic*, or bat people. Their origin story relates that their ancestors once discovered a bat (*zotz*, pronounced *soj*) made of stone, and came to see it as their god. Ever since, they've considered the bat—really a bat-human, as their sculptures from their earliest times show—to be the guardian of the underworld and as such, a powerful and potent force against their enemies.

"Really, there's no separation between the dark and light sides, the good and the evil," she says. "Not everyone does evil, but everyone can do it, under certain circumstances. You, too, Christopher. *Zotzilaha* is our reminder that if certain evil things happen to us or those we love, we might can do evil ourselves, even some of us who usually have great inner strength."

She then says, "Your light shines through, Christopher. And you're strong. The one you describe is weak. Scared. Unable to care for himself and those he's supposed to care for and take care of."

We get up from the bench. I nod my head toward the *templo*. "Will you play something for me?"

"After you left, my little brother would go there with me," she says. "He'd dance along as I played. I don't go there anymore. Now I play guitar."

Veruch then tells me of the love she has in her life, the father of her child, who taught her to play it during his time away from working in the *milpa*. What she shares brings to mind something I read when I was twelve in *Boy's Life* magazine—the January 1972 issue to be exact (I know because I clipped out the article and put it in my scrapbook). It relates that Socrates had played the lute, precursor to the guitar. The article says, "Homer and Socrates played this stringed instrument in ancient Greece. Later players included Martin Luther, Queen Elizabeth, and Johann Sebastian Bach." If it was good enough for those exemplary souls, it was good enough for me. While I lived in San Cristobal, I resumed lessons after my wife gave me a guitar for Christmas.

I promise Veruch before we part company that night that I will bring my guitar with me when I next return, and this time with all my family.

"Remember that good deed that you shared with me," she says. "The person who did that good deed has taken a dark path, and is gone. But the deed lives on."

PIANO MAN

In his poem *Yesterdays*, the celebrated Argentinian essayist, short story writer, and poet Jorge Luis Borges writes,

> From a lineage of Protestant ministers, and South American soldiers who fought, with their incalculable dust, against the Spaniards and the desert's lances, I am and I am not.

In my case, from a lineage of maritime people, philanthropists, misanthropes, murderers and thieves, heroes and antiheroes, who fought with their incalculable volcanic ash, against the Turks, Italians, Persians, Germans, and fellow Greeks and the island of Nisyros's long sarissa spears, swords, armor, shields, phalanxes, ballistae, and warships, I am and I am not.

"My true lineage," Borges goes on, "is the voice, that I still hear, of my father." He recalls how his father read to him works by the erotic taboo-breaking poet and novelist Algernon Charles Swinburne of the Victorian era. My father, on the other hand, crooned to me while playing the daylights out of the warped piano he'd owned since his youth and that he'd toted with him ever since. With yours truly as his enrapt audience, he wrestled out of it a series of suggestively sultry, bawdy Greek ballads and boogie-woogie tunes that in one way or another sprang both from his heritage and from America's Deep South.

I hear now the voice of my father more than ever. When playing and singing, Dad was unselfconscious in a way he couldn't afford to be in his professional life, this diminutive, swarthy, high-level federal official, a ship designer and award-winning electrical engineer with an at times pronounced lisp who successfully navigated the at-times backstabbing minefields of the mission-critical Department of Defense. Away from work, Dad lost himself, and found himself, in his piano playing—much as I do, and I imagine Socrates did, in our philosophical music-making.

My father had a rhythm and cadence all his own. It was evident in the way he carried himself—a jauntiness, a swagger, a joy. It was evident whenever he made music, Dad's entire body taken over by the beat, the picture of ecstatic joy, both utterly within and outside himself.

MUSIC MAN

Friedrich Nietzsche famously says in *The Birth of Tragedy* that what the modern world needed was a "Socrates as music-maker," and that this would be a sure sign of our advancement and evolution as individuals and a species. Nietzsche did not believe that the original Socrates himself was such a music maker. It's as if he hadn't read the *Republic*, in which Socrates extols the spirit of *sophrosyne* that "stretches through the whole, from top to bottom of the entire scale, making the weaker, the stronger, and those in the middle . . . sing the same chant together."

The noted Romanian philosopher and essayist E. M. Cioran, on the other hand, gets that the historical Socrates was a music maker in his own right. Cioran points out in *Drawn and Quartered* that while Socrates's hemlock was being prepared, he "was learning how to play a new tune on the flute":

"What will be the use of that?" he was asked. "To know this tune before dying." If I dare repeat this reply long since trivialized by the handbooks, it is because it seems to me the sole serious justification of any desire to know, whether exercised on the brink of death or at any other moment of existence.

Socrates scripted his own death every bit as much as he did his life. His dying words and works were his swan song. Socrates was all about attunement. His evocative inquiries were riffs and improvisations with whiffs of jazz that at their crescendos oozed cadence, rhythm, soul—musicality, in a word. He was both a composer and a song unto himself.

Though Nietzsche was himself a music-making and music-practicing philosopher (he played piano and violin; composed music for voice, piano, and violin; and wrote startling lyrical poetry), he mischaracterizes Socrates as someone who did not possess such arts and artfulness. Yet Socrates's entire body of work was an homage to and expression of them.

There's also this: Socrates's reason for being emerged from his encounter with the prophetess at Delphi. He was ensconced in an atmosphere of dance and drug and poetry, rhythm and frenzy fueled in part by gaseous fumes emanating from fissures in the earth. In those days, all were considered ideal elements that contributed to and even constituted the ingredients of music making itself. Entranced in that heady, intoxicating temple, Socrates had the epiphany that the walls between the rational and the mad, the poetic and discursive, were not necessarily at cross-purposes, and could be of a piece. The Socrates of the *Phaedrus*, an admix of Plato and Socrates (surely Plato thought he was doing more, not less, justice to his mentor's own perspectives in these latter works of his), says that

there is also a madness which is a divine gift, and the source of the chiefest blessings granted to men. For prophecy is a madness, and the prophetess at Delphi and the priestess at Dodona [another principal shrine] when out of their senses have conferred great benefits on Hellas [continental Greece], both in public and private life. . . . [P]rophecy which foretells the future . . . is the noblest of arts, with . . . an inspired madness which is a noble thing. . . . [T]he madness of love is the greatest of heaven's blessings.

Not to mention they conferred "great benefits" to Socrates himself. This is not at all to say that where reason ends, one should feel free to take a leap into the irrational, the mystical, the mad; rather, there is no such thing as pure reason, and reason at its most loving and creative can be interweaved with, among other things (like moral imagination), elements of divine, inspired madness.

Another latter masterpiece of Plato's, *Phaedo*, also takes place in the immediate time preceding Socrates's suicide, while the hemlock is being prepared for him. Now far removed from the hurly-burly, surrounded by nearest and dearest, he at last can take some pause. Socrates composes songs, writes poetry. The lyrics and poems he penned include a "prelude" to the god Apollo, whom the oracle at Delphi served. At the end of his life, as this dialogue tells it, Socrates is giving himself up fully to the muse. He has next to no time, and all the time in the world.

Socrates says this about himself in *Gorgias*: "It would be better for me that my lyre or a chorus I directed should be out of tune and loud with discord, and that multitudes of men should disagree with me rather than that my single self should be out of harmony with myself and contradict me." He was considered discordant by the false prophets of his day who cried, "Peace, peace" when there was no peace, but completely at harmony with himself because he adhered to his moral code and convictions and spoke truth to power. He was in effect a loud, out-of-tune human lyre, sentenced to death for breaking laws that made it a capital crime to call out the human liars who were dooming democracy.

PRICELESS RENDEZVOUS IN SAO PAULO

"*Saudade*," Sonia says to me at a Cuban café in the heart of Sao Paulo, Brazil.

The eighteen-year-old had attended the keynote talk I gave earlier in the day in Sao Paulo, Brazil, at an eminent business ethics conference. Among other professional hats, I'm an investment advisor representative, and enjoy philosophizing about—and putting into actual investment practice—sustainable, responsible, impact investing. Little wonder, given my father's lifelong passion for and expertise in investing, since his early twenties. Socrates himself was also a key inspiration; he pontificates stirringly, in Xenophon's final essay, on how to properly and fruitfully manage an estate, on what true wealth really amounts to, and on the virtuous use of money and other worldly possessions.

Here in Brazil's most populated city, I spoke to an audience of five hundred or so about how the most important quality of any society, regardless of the type of economy it promulgates, is its capacity to be self-critical. By that I mean that it must go out of its way to encourage a culture that promotes intensive, informed, honest dialogue that exposes and examines its faults, perils, more inhumane tendencies. I told them that whether society is one based on Marxian tenets, on fast-paced capitalism, fashioned on notions from Plato's *Republic*, or a curious mixture of many kinds of economies, what matters most is that it compels a citizenry to be relentlessly honest about itself, with the end of then coming up with ways to recognize and counter its darker dispositions. Clearly, this requires a society with a considerable degree of openness, and of courage, since the outcome of such honesty scrutiny can spark its radical restructuring.

Unbeknown to most on hand, I was operating on pure adrenaline; I'd barely had a chance to adjust to the time change after the ten-thousand-kilometer journey (about sixty-two hundred miles) that started out from Athens, much less to consider with calm my cousin Calliope's exhortation and charge to seek out, in some earnest, how to love the unlovable, forgive the unforgivable, and at the same time, come to better knowledge and understanding about myself, in ways that might resonate with others. What with an hours-long delay on my connecting flight, it was time for me to take to the stage and speak here not long after I arrived.

The audience response to my talk was gratifying, especially the questions the young people attending grilled me with afterward. Most indicated that they believed that the new conservative federal government and the free market policies it endorsed were a breath of fresh air. Their hopes had risen, only to be dashed, when the socialist-leaning Workers Party had taken over the reins of power in 2003 when they were kids, only for its leaders, one after the other, to become captive to greed, power, and corruption. One of them, Filipe, quoted John Emerich Edward Dalberg-Acton, the nineteenth-century English historian, writer, and politician who observed that "power tends to corrupt, and absolute power corrupts absolutely. Great men are almost always bad men." Sonia then said (presciently, it would turn out), that she had little doubt that the newest government would end up the same way as its predecessors, with all their initial high hopes turning out to be groundless and deceptive—but that, be that as it may, she and most everyone else in her generation were determined to speak truth to power, because it was the only way they'd ever be able to realize their aspirations in their personal and private lives.

Sonia and a number of other public high school students between ages sixteen and eighteen had garnered scholarships to attend the pretty pricey conference; they were chosen for their exceptional academic excellence as well as their admirable efforts in the workaday world. While they'd spent the intensive day rubbing shoulders with well-respected business leaders and ethics scholars from Brazil and the world over, they were not in any way cowed or in awe, and asked astute, piercing questions of all of us who were keynote speakers and panelists.

Mine turned out to be such a meaningful give-and-take that it prompted the program hosts to ask me if I'd also facilitate, at the end of the conference, a Socrates Café—on the question "What is priceless?"

Sonia was among the first to speak up during our philosophical exchange. "For me, what's most priceless is learning how to gain the tools I need to accomplish what I hope to in life." She shared that she has dyslexia and attention deficit hyperactivity disorder, which weren't diagnosed until she was well into her teen years. "My early years were hell for me and my family. I thought I was going crazy. My parents couldn't afford to send me to a specialist. It wasn't until I got a full-time job after school at age sixteen that qualified me for private health care that I finally was diagnosed correctly.

"I no longer think I'm nuts. Now I have an ADHD coach helping me educate myself on how my brain works and how it differs from the normal person. Just the revelation that I'm not neurotypical was a relief. It wasn't anything that I was doing wrong that kept me from performing well in school. My brain's workings are entirely different from that of most people. I'm learning how to apply that knowledge, and navigate whatever task is given me or goal I have. My learning disabilities will never go away, but now I can map out strategies to succeed that take into account the unique workings of my brain. I've been able to gain confidence and achieve a level of satisfaction and success that I wasn't able to all the previous years in my life. I'm an honors student accepted with full scholarship at a prestigious university, on my way." She smiled. "As that commercial says, 'Priceless.'"

Everyone—everyone—stood up and clapped for her.

Sonia and several other students had more to say even after the hour allotted for our dialogue had passed, and I wanted to listen and learn. We gravitated to a nearby twenty-four-hour Cuban café to continue philosophizing and chatting, while drinking strong, bitter coffee.

Sonia and the rest of those seated around a circular table live about an hour and a half away—at least, by the time they take a series of labyrinthine bus connections—from where we are in the tonier section of the city. They tell me that their *favela*—one of countless massive unregulated informal settlements in Brazil that low- and middle-income citizens have established—is very much a close-knit neighborhood, not at all the dangerous place that one reads about.

Sonia shares with me more of her story that night. She tells me her full-time job after school has made it possible for her employer to deduct enough from her paycheck to provide health coverage for her parents and brother, who'd otherwise be dependent on the public health care system, a shambles of mediocrity and ineptitude with scarce critical medical supplies. She also shares that her goal is to work in the field of sustainable development. She has the high hope of matriculating in the vaunted Earth Institute program at Columbia University, and then returning to Brazil to dedicate her energies to preserving the Amazon.

I'm not sure how or why—chalk it up to her uncanny ability to get me sharing things I'd never planned to, along with my emotional and physical exhaustion interlaced with exhilaration over being in this city, if only for one full day, and having such an intensive, meaningful visit—but at some point I share with Sonia some of the slings and arrows I've experienced since my father's death.

The single Portuguese word that Sonia says after I'm finished is, "*Saudade.*"

She meets my quizzical look with this: "There's no literal translation for it to another language. It's so many things—grief and soul and loss and love and mourning and desperation and yearning.

"You grieve for your father, and yes, you grieve for what might have been if someone decent had been there to intervene his last days," she then says. "But that's not the only reason you have the longing and yearning and absence that is *saudade*. You feel *saudade* over betrayal by someone you and your father trusted completely.

"Your dad, you long for him, too, wish you hadn't taken some things for granted, hadn't judged him so fiercely. He's always present; that makes his absence even more painful. You'll always be saying your goodbyes to your father, and this person who betrayed you both."

What this uncommonly perceptive person says has the jarring ring of honest insight. We are silent for a long while. Then I say, "I also have *saudade* for the family that might have been in my young days. It had so much promise. But it never lived up to it."

I then look at my watch. It is nearly 5:00 a.m. now. I have to rush back to my hotel, pack my few belongings, then streak to the airport about 25 kilometers away. I tell Sonia I would never have understood this vital part of what I longed and yearned for and mourned over if not for her.

"I have to get something for you," she says. As Sonia rushes out of the café, she calls out to me, "I'll meet you at the lobby of your hotel."

I wait first in the lobby and then outside the hotel entrance. I tell my impatient Uber driver to start charging me while I wait for Sonia and look repeatedly at my watch. I don't have the heart to leave, and don't have her number to call her. I finally have no choice but to get in the car, lest I miss my flight. Sonia at last arrives, breathless. She has a look on her face that is the furthest from disappointment. She hands me a book with a musty, faded cover. A collection of poems from Carlos Drummond de Andrade, Brazil's most revered poet who died in 1987 at age eighty-five.

As appreciative and touched as I am, I tell her I have to leave immediately. But before I can, she takes my wrist to waylay me, opens the book hastily to a page, and reads the beginning of a poem of Drummond de Andrade's titled "A Um Ausente."

> Tenho razão de sentir saudade, tenho razão de te acusar. Houve um pacto implícito que *rompeste. e sem te despedires foste embora.*

> I am right to miss you, I am right to accuse you. There was an implicit pact that you broke. and without saying goodbye you left.

"You will never get over this *saudade*," she says. "How can you? Why would you? Though in very different ways, not one person, but two people left you without saying proper goodbyes. This is a yearning and mourning, a grieving and longing that goes too deep. It's part of you now, forever. I can tell even in the brief time I've known you—a lifetime in a day and a night and a day again—that you will experience not just renewed joy from this, but a new kind of joy. In your presentation at the conference, you spoke with such passion about the people at life's extremes that you have dialogues with, how you learn from their wisdom—a wisdom that you said often springs from indescribable heartbreak. And yet, you said to all of us, most of them somehow still have this aura of joy about them, they're so full of love, and caring, that life hasn't beaten them down.

"This world, it's in the heart-breaking business," this wise young soul says to me now, her hazel eyes sparkling. "Your joyful nature can't be separated from your tears and heartbreak, Christopher. Your heart is strong. Keep loving. Keep allowing your heart to be broken."

Sonia gives me a tight embrace, a light brush of a kiss—a mere wisp on the cheek—and I am off.

A VAGUE AND CONSTANT DESIRE

Saudade entered the Portuguese lexicon in the thirteenth century. In that era, hundreds of thousands sailed in Portuguese ships to other parts of South America, to Africa and Asia, North America and Europe, in search of a better life. All who set off on such journeys knew they were fraught with uncertainty and risk. Their loved ones to whom they bid their farewells in particular felt a longing and yearning, a regret and sorrow. They knew that the odds were steep that their beloveds would return, that it was far more probable they would die in shipwrecks and battles and of disease, or would simply disappear without a trace for reasons unknown. Those left behind suffered enormously from the void that in too many instances proved to be lasting ones. The keen felt presence of the profound absence of someone beloved now gone forevermore, is *saudade*. The word springs from the Latin *solitates*, or solitudes. Far more than mere grief-induced melancholy or nostalgia, it is a longing and a lacking that never goes away; to the contrary, it deepens with the passing of time.

In his 1912 book *Portugal*, the literary scholar and translator A. F. G. Bell writes that *saudade* "is a vague and constant desire for something that does not and probably cannot exist, for something other than the present, a turning towards the past or towards the future; not an active discontent or poignant sadness but an indolent dreaming wistfulness." Neto Coelho, the Brazilian writer and politician who founded the Brazilian Academy of Letters, calls *saudade* "the memory of the heart." Carlos Drummond de Andrade seems to have a conception of *saudade* that is a blend of these perspectives: "We also have *saudades* of what did not exist."

Had I experienced *saudade* my first visit to Nisyros? I felt my father's presence and absence with an acute wistfulness and longing, regret and . . . joy—for the relationship of ours that was, for the one that never was and likely never would have been, even if Dad had lived a thousand more years, for the relationship that was coming to pass that stemmed from the wondrous week he and I spent, the spring before his death, bonding anew and sharing confidences in a way we'd never done before, and for the relationship I have with him now. But I also feel a void and grief for another relationship that now is stymied by unimaginable betrayal.

LOST IN TRANSLATION

Several difficult-to-translate Hellenic Greek terms that were central to Socrates's quest have been repeatedly mistranslated, and hence woefully misunderstood, for centuries on end—key among them are *sophrosyne*, *eudaimonia*, *daimon*, and *arete*. This has precipitated scandalous misrepresentations of the philosopher's ultimate aims. All of these terms, just as with *saudade*, have moral and spiritual dimensions and require imaginative vision if one is to make ideal use of them in one's own life and times.

Saudade is not inward brooding or past-dwelling per se; it has a forward-looking dimension that can be used to make more real an imagined present. I might mourn and long for a family that never was or could be, a family that had one too many decided elements of Greek and Shakespearean tragedy. Perhaps this is in large part why, for so long as an adult, I kept committed relationships at arm's length. Then one fall 1996 day, when I was thirty-seven and orchestrating a Socrates Café on the question "What is love?" I bared my deepest fears (and hopes) to the only person who showed up besides me. She looked at me with love and understanding and told me that I'm not among those who are doomed to be prisoners of past hurts and wounds, familial and otherwise. With the all-encompassing power of her love and belief in me, I confronted and overcame fears that long had held me in grip. With her, I now have a family of my own choosing. Me, my wife Ceci, and our two daughters are not a perfect family (whatever that might mean), but we communicate openly and honestly even when it hurts, as we seek to become ever more loving and understanding of each other, and help one another discover our passions and pursue them with all our being. We are the opposite of the family of moats and chasms and walls in which I lamentably grew up.

Saudade is kindred to "Socratic *eudaimonia*," a joy that one experiences alongside loss, heartbreak, despair. It is the buoyant spirit that emerges from dealing with and channeling the worst slings and arrows, that compels you to keep on keeping on more than ever, not as an end in itself but with renewed purpose, and with a clearer notion of how to do your part to make ours a more loving world. Even though you're no longer completely unbowed or unbroken, out of your suffering, you muster even more grit, more spirit and determination to weather the thousand natural (and unnatural) shocks that come your way—not for the puny, selfish end of "well, I'll show those bastards that they can't keep me down," but with imaginative vision and ethical wisdom that makes it more probable you'll take concrete steps to lessen the preventable hurts inflicted on and by the world.

To do this, one must also incorporate and put into action other hard-to-translate terms from Socrates's day—*sophrosyne*, *eudaimonia*, and *arete*.

Sophrosyne, far more often than not, is mistranslated as moderation or temperance, when what it means is knowing when to hold on, when to let go, when to restrain yourself (and perhaps others), when not to, with the end of achieving greater self and societal openness and liberation; it can only be achieved with rather relentless seeking of self-knowledge and self-awareness. *Eudaimonia*, in its right, is not mere happiness, as commonly misportrayed, but joyousness, and of a kind that comes to be after experiencing profound agony, suffering, despair, which (if you survive such experience) is the brew out of which you are endowed with greater empathy, understanding, as well as humane, forward-looking vision. Its bedfellow *daimon* is no otherworldly voice, but one that emerges, more often than not at a young age, along with the kindred spirit of *atopos*—not alienation, but "misfit-ness"—from feeling out of place and, as a consequence, pondering deeply what nature and self and your place in the scheme of things are all about. *Arete* is scandalously translated as virtue, cheapening and diluting both concepts and causing legion distortions of who and what Socrates was all about and what a modern iteration of his practice might amount to today. *Arete* is in fact the ceaseless striving for excellence in all of life's dimensions, an aspirational component interwoven with a decided moral clarion call in which duty to self and others goes hand in glove; this makes it incumbent to "live like Socrates," or put another way, to live the "life of should."

These concepts have an existential dimension. The spirit of *saudade*, when combined with the spirits of *sophrosyne, eudaimonia, daimon, atopos,* and *arete*, should inspire you never (or rarely) to take a moment for granted. They make you realize, as Hillel the Elder, the Jewish religious leader, sage, and scholar, puts it, "If I am not for myself, who will be for me? And being for myself, what am 'I'? And if not now when?" This sentiment must be applied in tandem with Hillel's other famous moral ukase, one that is far more powerful than what we mistake today to be the Golden Rule: "That which is hateful to you, do not do to your fellow." Rather than doing unto others what you believe you would want done unto you, you do *not* do unto others anything you yourself would find abhorrent.

If not now, when? If not me, who?

This does not mean becoming so devoted to a mission or cause or movement that you live every moment at a frenetic, breakneck, almost out-of-body pace, but relishing your time here and your times with, and without, those you love. It means even relishing your defeats, and shaping something meaningful out of them—most always with the understanding that this life shall pass quickly, even if we live to be a hundred.

As Rainer Maria Rilke puts it in "The Ninth Elegy" of his *Duino Elegies*, "Everyone *once, once* only. Just *once* and no more. And we also *once* . . . But this having been *once*, . . . to have been of the earth seems irrevocable." If you subscribe to this "Socratic outlook," all the more reason to make the heartfelt attempt to sculpt and mold something meaningful that makes the world prospectively more livable and lovable for one and all, in part out of the terrifically grievous loss of those you loved who are no longer here, and in part out of the terrifically grievous loss of those still here but who nonetheless are out of reach.

LESSONS BEFORE AND AFTER DYING

My father's death is a cross to bear. The pain over his loss has at times pushed me to the tipping point. Senseless and tragic occurrences happen every minute of every day; I know that. The preponderance of these befall the world's most vulnerable and fragile, with the elderly, like my father at the time of his death, among the most victimized.

Even so, matters are seldom cut and dried when it comes to "bad" or "evil" things happening to "good" people. What constitutes a good or a bad person, much less a purely good or bad one, much less a saintly or an evil person, can be relational to culture, to ever-shifting ethical criteria, belief systems, epoch, ideals. While there are those rare transcendent souls who by most any benchmark are deemed "good," there are also occasions when even such a person as that can all of a sudden "snap" and do something horrible, for any number of reasons (or lack thereof). Conversely, some who commit monstrous deeds have also shown loving-kindness. Someone may have at times been a loving father, see his progeny as his one and only decent accomplishment, even if an unrepentant wrongdoer in most other ways. Such a person may do anything—anything—to save face with his own child, even if there are also other motives and drives, including insatiable greed. On the other hand, some who are considered godly have dark impulses. They may be able to conceal them (even from themselves) but not altogether contain or control them, and may cause untold harm to innocents in their orbit.

In most cases, our disposition to label others in black-and-white moralistic and judgmental terms overlooks the murkier, more nuanced, complex facets that can only be teased out if you take considerable time to flesh out the details of anyone's story. It is the only way to breach the walls of prejudice and (mis)judgment we hold toward others. Labeling and judging, too often, are primarily attempts to deflect judgment from oneself. So easy to label someone in the harshest terms, including "sociopath" and "psychopath." So hard to ask: What about me? What about society? What about all those who live in a world of plenty, when they well know that millions of others are dying of malnutrition and pestilence and preventable illness, when they well know (or should) that a billion of their fellow humans don't have access to a basic facility to wash their hands—an act that can kill germs, bacteria, viruses that might otherwise be fatal (especially during a pandemic)? What about those who are aware of this and do little or nothing about it? What about those who shed not a tear over this unjust state of affairs? What about those who know that it is always the poorest who are most often maimed or killed in violent conflicts not of their making that are orchestrated by the powerful, and do little or nothing to speak out about, much less remedy, this unjust state of affairs? Such people would be well served to ask themselves if they have something of the sociopath in them, and if their society in whole cloth reflects a profound pathology.

A human being, more often than not, has ample doses both of virtue and vice. A father, for instance, may be an exemplary bread-winner, have a work ethic second to none, yet devote nary a thought to setting a moral example for his kids. He may be admir-ably thrifty to the extreme, saving and investing every spare penny over many decades, in part to see to it that those he most loves and believes most deserving don't have to fret so much financially. Yet he may also unscrupulously hide his finances from prying eyes, and even enlist the help of amoral others to do so—others who might, if they learn they are cut off from his trove, say, because of their litany of acts of fraud (perhaps influenced by a father's own un-glowing example), take matters into their own hands and do what-ever necessary to take what they have convinced themselves is their just deserts. A father may be a genuine and inveterate social and civic entrepreneur, widely admired and looked up to for good rea-son in that regard. He may be a most protective husband of a fragile spouse. Yet he may also be a flagrant womanizer (contributing to his spouse's fragility). He may, behind closed doors, have an un-predictable temper, even lash out against defenseless kids who have done no wrong, just because he can—perhaps angry at not leading a life of his choosing—and wants to vent. He may betray a withering schadenfreude to a child under his wing who commits blunder upon transgression upon blunder, never learning any lessons (perhaps incapable of doing so), never accepting an iota of responsibility. Yet he may also be the first to provide succor, again and again. This is not to say that a person is a bundle of contradictions—only that too many lack the awareness (or the desire to have awareness) of those contradictions that keep people and their society (including their family society) from flourishing fully. Because such flourishing takes mordant honesty, imaginative vision, and the creation of a concrete strategy to realize that vision to become more than we are as individuals and a society at any given moment.

Family tragedies abound. So do triumphs. Most go unrecorded, even if and as the works and deeds that result from them continue to reverberate. Some overcome the circumstances they couldn't control while growing up and surmount even the gravest hurts that came their way. They go on to live genuinely creative, meaningful, and most of all decent lives, free of most resentment and hence liberated from all that came before, not just showing that you can overcome your past, but give new meaning to it. Others crash and burn, and try with all their might to bring down others with them.

How *do* you handle, as Hamlet puts it, the "heartache, and the thousand natural shocks that flesh is heir to"? In act 3, scene 1, Hamlet holds that the central human conundrum is "whether 'tis nobler in the mind to suffer the slings and arrows of outrageous fortune, or to take arms against a sea of troubles." The choice need not be either-or. Or at least, it depends on what "taking up arms" can mean. In navigating the Scylla and Charibdis of such shocks and troubles, you don't have to suffer with passive resignation, and you don't have to take up arms in a physical way. You might instead consider, as Veruch taught me, how those who would do things evil also did or do some good toward others in their lives, perhaps including you yourself. This might spur you on, more than ever, to leave your own legacy of goodness, with greater drive and duty than ever—and to do so in part on behalf of all those who didn't, wouldn't, or can't.

Legacies more often than not are a mixed bag, and even the most well intentioned of efforts to "do some good" can go miserably awry. Perhaps one's words and works and deeds may only be judged or gauged with the passage of time. Often a great deal of time. And never once and for all.

With his closest friends and companions, Dad spoke in unreserved, glowing terms—in a way that was hard for him to do directly with me—of the lasting legacy of goodness he believed I was leaving the world. It does give me some sense of release that he left this world feeling that way, even if I'm not sure what, if anything, my legacy might amount to. I do know this: whatever I try to accomplish that does some good, I do so also on behalf of those who've made a concerted yet (so far) failed attempt to crush my spirit. It is an undeniable hurt to have been denied the chance to say my goodbyes to my father. And as someone who lives on a wing and a prayer, as my father well knew, it is only human to wonder what I could have done with the financial bounty he'd worked so hard for so long to leave me. But I gladly would have handed over every penny of that sizable inheritance just to have been able to say goodbye to him.

I wasn't given the chance to have that choice. Yet this has spurred me to redouble my efforts to leave a positive footprint. More than ever I want to do my modest bit, one of the walking wounded with an unbowed determination to make my daughters' world a saner and safer place for them and all other children, and so help heal the preventable hurts of the world. I try to do this not just for Dad, or my own daughters, but also on behalf of those who are too wounded, and too bent on wounding others, to leave a caring and loving footprint themselves.

ENCOUNTER AT THE OFFICE OF BROTHER CORNEL WEST

The imposing ornate Gothic architecture of the Harvard Divinity School's exterior contrasts with the more warm and welcoming interior. I'm here to meet with the revered scholar, author, activist, and public intellectual Dr. Cornel West. I've never known anyone more filled with love and wonder, honesty and integrity—moral, spiritual, intellectual—than Brother West, author of the classic *Race Matters*, which if anything is more relevant now even than when it was first published in 1993, and its sequel, *Democracy Matters*.

Both a devout Christian of the prophetic Judaic tradition and an inveterate practitioner of the Socratic way of interrogation (what with "its ontological dizziness and existential vertigo")—Dr. West believes each tradition serves as a vital "corrective" to the other— he walks the walk each and every day, spending himself utterly, to bring about a more open, loving, caring, and sharing world on all scales. If he has his way, ours will one day be a humanity without borders. As I've witnessed time and again over the eight years that I've known him at the time of this latest encounter, Brother West engages all human beings as equals, no matter their age, stage, or station; he brings everyone with whom he is engaged into his orbit, as he all the while steps wholly into theirs.

I had arrived late the previous evening from Portland, Oregon, where I'd had a commitment right after my visit to San Cristobal de las Casas in Chiapas, Mexico. There had been a knife attack on that city's public transit system that left two Muslim women dead and another wounded. Racial and ethnic tensions were on the rise. I'd been asked to hold a Socrates Café on bridging the divides of race and prejudice. A professor who had ventured there with some of his students from neighboring Washington State, and who was clearly full of himself, said near the outset, "I wish I could spend all my time killing white racists," a comment that met with his students' applause, and that of some others. How do you overcome racism and its evil twins, classism and elitism, when you don't, can't, see that you are more part of the problem than the solution? The walls of political division between and among Americans today are unprecedented. The word *polarization* doesn't do justice to what is happening in my country right now. Another participant read my mind: a woman stood up and said, her voice shaking and full of emotion, "I'm a transplant here, from Ann Arbor. I was there the day in 1996 that an eighteen-year-old African American teen, Keshia Thomas, saved a member of the Ku Klux Klan who was taking part in a white supremacist rally from being beaten to death by 'progressives.' It wasn't enough for them to tear up his Confederate flag. Not enough to run him off. They shouted, 'Kill the Nazi' and proceeded to beat him to a pulp. Who knows what led that KKK member to become fed with such hateful poison. But the progressives were just as poisonous." She looked at the professor, "So you stuff that sanctimonious shit up your ass before you breed another generation of killers." He was red faced, and silent, in the face of loud and sustained applause. I had not known of Keshia Thomas but learned considerably more about her after our dialogue, researching her on the internet during my cross-country plane flight. "Someone had to step out of the pack and say, 'this isn't right,'" she said in an interview I came across online. "I knew what it was like to be hurt. The many times that that happened, I wish someone would have stood up for me . . . violence is violence—nobody deserves to be hurt, especially not for an idea." Months later, Keshia Thomas received a visit from a young man. He told her that the person whose life she saved was his father, and that he just wanted to thank her from the bottom of his heart. A student journalist who took a powerful photograph of Ms. Thomas shielding the racist from further harm said, "She put herself at physical risk to protect someone who, in my opinion, would not have done the same for her. Who does that in this world?"

Who does that in this world? While everyone else stood idly by or looked the other way—everyone else who wasn't pummeling the white supremacist—Keshia Thomas did the right thing. I left Portland both energized and concerned that too many of us are looking the other way, just as they did in Socrates's time, and with a redoubled commitment to speak out whenever wrongs were occurring before my very eyes.

It is in this time and clime that I arrive for my latest meetup with Brother West. The towering intellect, social critic, and humanist has dedicated his life to confronting and overcoming those elements in self and society that prevent us from living and loving without borders; Cornel West wants to set us free, and he stresses that we each have a role and responsibility in making that happen. As he inimitably puts it in *Race Matters*:

> To be a jazz freedom fighter is to attempt to galvanize and energize world-weary people into forms of organization with accountable leadership that promote critical exchange and broad reflection. The interplay of individuality and unity is not one of uniformity and unanimity imposed from above but rather of conflict among diverse groupings that reach a dynamic consensus subject to questioning and criticism. As with a soloist in a jazz quartet, quintet or band, individuality is promoted in order

> to sustain and increase the creative tension with the group. . . .
> This kind of critical and democratic sensibility flies in the face
> of any policing of borders and boundaries of "blackness,"
> "maleness," "femaleness," or "whiteness."

I arrive early at Dr. West's office for our latest get-together. He is still holding office hours for his students. One of them is occupying the wooden bench directly outside his office. When the young man seated in the middle of the bench sees me, he hastily closes up various books he has opened on each side of him, picks them up, and stacks them on the floor. He moves to one end of the bench and gestures for me to sit down.

Just as I am set to sit down, he stands up and shakes my hand vigorously. "I'm Kigaso," he says. "It's a Zulu name. It means 'peace.'" Kigaso tells me that this is the second of his third year as a graduate divinity student.

He cuts to the chase: "Who are you? How do you know Dr. West? What are you doing here?"

I get no further than relating that I'm the author of a trilogy of books about my adventures and misadventures holding Socrates Cafés the world over when he interrupts: "I read one of your books!" His eyes are almost as wide with astonishment as mine. "*You* are Christopher Phillips. I read your *Socrates in Love* after Dr. West told me about it." He again shakes my hand, even more vigorously if possible.

"In that book, you write about the dialogues you had in South Africa. You know, your encounters with people in Soweto, near where I'm from, they give people there hope," Kigaso tells me. "I'm not surprised by how welcoming people in Soweto were to you. A lot of black South Africans, especially in the ghetto, never experience white people—white South Africans, much less white Americans—who willingly come to where they live, to meet with them and learn from them like you did.

"You saw for yourself the levels of extreme poverty and the extreme levels of wealth—the rich living side by side with the poor. You approach the poorest with so much humility. You make it clear you don't have an agenda except to inquire with them, to listen, to learn. So people let down their guard. You know, black South Africans, ever since Nelson Mandela was freed from prison at Robben Island in 1990 after twenty-seven years there—he said we needed to become 'a rainbow nation at peace with itself and the world'—have been looking for opportunities for white people to come and see how they live. It's so important for white people to stray from their comfort zones into black people's discomfort zones.

"The circle dialogues you hold are very similar to our original tribal democratic traditions that involve everyone and that require everyone to say not just what they think, but why they think what they do. We wouldn't call it 'Socratic' but it's kindred.

"The one thing that the world is missing is knowledge of African mythology. Everyone knows about Greek mythology, about the Western Empire, about the Asian Empire, okay, fine. But the one thing that's missing is what *you* relate in your book, Christopher Phillips: the gathering of South Africans around the fire, tribal members gathering, for storytelling, wisdom sharing, imparting ancient knowledge.

"So, when you yourself, someone who has both Greek and American citizenship, come to a place like Soweto, where the poor from so many provinces have flocked to, looking for economic opportunity, when you come as you do and as you are, to inquire with us, you emulate our own traditions, drawing from our well of being, from our own lived experience. You draw our stories from us out of our marrow about who we are and what we're all about. That is so significant."

Then Kigaso says, "I'm studying world religions here in the graduate program. It is a joy each and every day to learn from Dr.

West, to have these incredible exchanges with him about James Baldwin, W. E. B. Du Bois, Lorraine Hansberry, Rabbi Abraham Joshua Heschel, Dr. Martin Luther King Jr., Malcolm X.

"It inspires me even more. When I return to South Africa, I'll continue challenging and revolutionizing the educational curriculum there. South African universities have endemic problems regarding equal access. We have launched a movement in South Africa called #FeesMustFall. One of the key elements in that protest in my country that I love so much is the decolonization of education. It is so important for people who have been oppressed to learn about their history. But since the dismantling of apartheid, the level of inequality in education persists, from preschool, to kindergarten, all the way up to high school and then private universities. It is still too much segregated by race, and by class."

I absorb every word of Kigaso's heartfelt, near-breathless soliloquy. Then he switches gears and says, "How do you know Dr. West?"

I tell him that Brother West, as I and so many others fondly call him, and I are going to record a Socratic give-and-take for a program I have that is part of our nonprofit Democracy Café–Socrates Café. I share with Kigaso that once, some years ago, when I was a senior writing and research fellow at the University of Pennsylvania teaching a course I'd developed on "Socratic Method and Democracy," I used Dr. West's *Democracy Matters* as a principal text, along with selected readings from his *Race Matters*. I had written to Brother West asking if he would speak to my students about his works via video teleconference. A week later, I received a phone call. It was from the dreaded "Unknown Caller." As a rule, I never answer such calls, almost always from telemarketers. But for some reason, I was drawn to answer, perhaps because it was the first anniversary of my father's death; I do not know.

"Is this Brother Christopher Phillips?"

The voice was unmistakable—sonorous yet somehow almost lilting, as if on the verge of breaking out into song at any moment. "Is this Brother Cornel West?"

"Indeed, indeed." It was our nation's foremost philosopher, his written and spoken words a mesmerizing blend of jazz, poetry, deep contemplativeness, passion for the just and the good, and an unsurpassable ability to draw connections among the most abiding knowledge traditions in ways that inspire one and all to be the change they want to see in the world at large. Dr. West told me he'd be happy and honored to accept my invitation to speak to my students—but not via video call with them; rather, he proposed to spend an entire day breaking bread with us, in person, and he offered also to be part of a gathering of the community at large at Penn and the Philadelphia community at large. We ironed out a date, and that was that.

My students were in as much a state of disbelief as I was that Brother West was coming, on his own nickel, to spend a full day with us. Two months later, he arrived early in the day from Princeton and gave every iota of himself to the engagements I'd arranged between him and my students, for the campus-wide community, and for denizens of the city of Philadelphia itself. We had give-and-takes with Dr. West to our hearts' content on Socrates, social responsibility, race and democracy matters, and how it is vital for all of us to be continually willing to challenge our own assumptions and prejudices.

I tell Kigaso that to this day, this gift Brother West gave hundreds of us during his visit to Philadelphia is of value beyond measure, and that this proved to be just the first occasion this human being, giving like no other, has held such exchanges with me. Dr. West and I have stayed in close touch ever since. I've never met a more genuine and unpretentious person, never met anyone more imbued with empathy and humility—and who as far as I can tell has not one drop of hate—than this man whose works will live on and on, long after, as he might put it, "we become the culinary delight of terrestrial worms."

What I do not share with Kigaso is that my most enduring and cherished memory of that magical day with Brother West in Philadelphia is when he and I shared a moment alone to have a bite to eat and a drink together; he caught me off guard when he said to me with feeling and yet matter-of-factly, "You're suffering, my brother."

Before I know it, I briefly related to him all the ugly and even mysterious circumstances surrounding my father's death.

Brother West got up, came over to me, and gave me a tight embrace. Sometime afterward, he said, "Never stop loving that person you're telling me about, my brother. There are those who spiritually do not receive the kind of love that they ought in their own families and communities and the larger societies. Never forget Dostoevsky's definition of love in *Brothers Karamazov*: hell is suffering from the incapacity to love. Such people think of themselves as so worthless, as not worthy of love.

"We know many people who do well financially who still hate themselves, and are still living in a psychic hell even though they have all the material things. On the other hand, we know many people who are spiritually rich, who are culturally rich, even though they are just as broke as the Ten Commandments financially."

And then: "Look at what you do, Brother Chris. You're helping people learn how to love—themselves and others. You create love-ins with your Socrates Café gatherings. Socrates never shed a tear, and Jesus never laughed. Two of our greatest teachers of virtue. But you've created a space where people can do both, and more."

The rest of the day, without a break (barely even to take a sip of water), Dr. West engaged my students, as well as the campus-wide and the greater Philadelphia community, in a series of give-and-takes on Socrates, democracy, and social responsibility. To bear witness as he spent himself entirely that day in his mission to make ours—by intimate personal example complemented by his soaring writing and activism—a more caring and connected world was an indelible experience for one and all.

Late that night, before he was set to leave and return to his home in Princeton, Dr. West and I briefly retreated to the building that houses my office. He stood out front on the porch, taking in the night air, as if he was in the country. He reminded me of a scene from one of Plato's dialogues in which Socrates is standing on a neighbor's porch, oblivious for a moment to everyone and everything. His driver eventually came to us and said, "Dr. West, we should be leaving now."

After one more embrace, Cornel West said to me, "Just remember, Brother Chris, remember always, part of your dad's afterlife is in your blessed life."

Ever since that first rendezvous with Brother West, I have never allowed myself to be nearly as captive to resentment or anger, much less animosity. Instead, I have been intent, even as I continue to strive to bring certain things to rights, to love those more than ever who are filled with malice and self-loathing and who themselves cannot love.

It is eight years since that experience with Brother West in Philly that I find myself talking with Kigaso outside his office. Just then, while I'm immersed in this rumination, Cornel West in the flesh emerges from his office. We share a hug. He's pleased to see that Kigaso and I have already hit it off in fine fashion. He says to his student, "Part of the framework of what I was trying to do in *Race Matters, Democracy Matters*, is so kindred in terms of the work that Brother Christopher has been doing for decades in terms of his own outreach and writing. The ways in which his calling and my own calling so profoundly overlap—that makes us more than friends, it makes us brothers; it makes us fellow questers for wisdom and fellow questers for justice and for truth and goodness and beauty."

Then Brother West says, "Brother Chris is an exemplary lover of wisdom, a lover of justice, a lover of the good, a lover of beauty—a free and autonomous human being. He has the courage to love. Not asking anybody's permission as to whom you love, and that flows from the depth of your soul." He gives me a knowing look, mixed with loving-kindness, as if recalling our tête-à-tête over lunch in Philadelphia, and then his parting words to me later that day, all those years ago.

Among an embarrassment of riches when it comes to enduring pearls of wisdom, Cornel West writes this in *Race Matters*:

> In these downbeat times, we need as much hope and courage as we do vision and analysis; we must accent the best of each other. . . . We are at a crucial crossroad in the history of this nation—and we either hang together by combating these forces that divide and degrade us or we hang separately. Do we have the intelligence, humor, imagination, courage, tolerance, love, respect, and will to meet the challenge? . . . None of us alone can save the nation or world. But each of us can make a positive difference if we commit ourselves to do so.

Brother West himself may hate indifference, may hate specific deeds; but he's the living embodiment of a person who does not hate any human being, no matter what he's said or done. He has set the highest of bars—one that, because of his example, inspires and leads me to make a renewed commitment when I awake each day to strive to be love filled, hate-less—to model by personal example the change I want to see in the world at large, a world that is crying out to be more lovable for one and all if it is ever to be more livable for one and all.

THE PHILOSOPHER'S STONE

I am at "my stone." Flat, mossy, expansive, it juts out on a smallish lake alongside a rural roadway several miles from the southeastern Maine hamlet where I once lived. It is in the heart of Maine's Lakes Region. Long the stepsister to the Pine Tree State's picturesque villages along the pristine, rocky coast, this is where I began my writing and teaching life.

After my latest visit with Cornel West, I made the two-hour train trip from Boston to Portland, then rented a car to drive another hour to the Lakes Region. The area is dotted with one lake after another. The unending economic expansion in the United States has at last extended its reach to this rural and—except summer months when city dwellers with second homes venture here, as do children and youth who attend the many camps in the area—relatively poorer part of New England. It has led to the rather unbridled construction of cookie-cutter housing developments and condo complexes just outside incorporated town bounds. Owned typically by the more well-to-do in the greater Boston and New York regions, they are distressingly out of place.

My stone itself, though, looks the exact same as when I first happened upon it decades ago. About fifteen feet in circumference, more or less in the shape of a parallelogram, with two jagged corners and two smooth ones, it has a large and inviting flat expanse. It almost serves the same purpose as a promontory, affording an in-the-round view of the area. The lake itself, though, has an unhealthy greenish tinge to it. In the months when the weather is good for extended stretches between late spring and midfall, too many now crowd it with their Jet Skis and motorboats. During the months in which the lake is frozen, however, and other times when mostly year-round residents are the only ones here, you still can feel as if all is right with this more sparse and tranquil Thoreauesque world. In the dead of winter, locals still push small homemade huts out toward the middle, cut a hole in the ice, and fish for brook, lake, brown and rainbow trout, landlocked salmon, large- and smallmouth bass, perch and pickerel.

Even when it isn't winter's acme, and the lake is not frozen, there are times when you can venture to my stone—such as today, a late-winter weekday when the weather is brisk but manageable—and experience utter silence as you gaze out on the lake and into yourself. This stone remains for me a go-to place to which I have been drawn over the decades whenever I am at a crossroads, threshold, or precipice in life. It is where I can, all at the same time, be in the now, in the then, and in the what's to come, fully present though not fully *in* the present.

Over time, as I sit or lie on the stone, its magic has its way with me, and I become transported. Not out of time or mind or body, just elsewhere. I can't honestly say where that is, only that I am not altogether here. When I am in its grip, I'm in a state of wonder and whimsy, of hereness and thereness and everywhereness that has little if anything to do with deliberate thinking and brooding, or, on the other hand, with deliberate nonthinking. This is no escape so much as it is a date with being and stillness and the ineffable that is far removed from the kind of contemplative attentiveness that characterizes mindfulness.

This is my place to be, most of all to be still. This is where my *daimon* comes to the fore, unbidden. Such is the wizardry of my philosopher's stone.

J. K. Rowling acquiesced to her U.S. publisher's request to change the title of her first book from *Harry Potter and the Philosopher's Stone* to *Harry Potter and the Sorcerer's Stone*. Yet a philosopher's stone is plenty magical—and unlike that of a sorcerer, it once was believed by some of the most respectable scientists in history to be real. Starting in the Middle Ages, all the way into the seventeenth century, the search was on to discover "the philosopher's stone." It was said to convert ordinary metals like iron, tin, lead, zinc into precious ones like gold and silver. It further was reputed to cure the gravest of illnesses, to serve as a medicinal fountain of youth that stopped and even reversed the aging process, and, holy grail of holy grails, to even confer the gift of immortality. Sir Isaac Newton himself, along with Robert Boyle, the founder of modern chemistry, for reasons no longer known—they must have been compelling ones for such luminaries to buy into the stone's existence—were among those who searched diligently for it. The problem and challenge was that the philosopher's stone was said to look like any other of its brethren of the more pedestrian variety, so the only way to find out if it was the real deal was to grind some of it and test it in laboratories. They did so, in vain, as did thousands of other scientists, never finding the chosen one.

Who knows, maybe this stone on which I'm sitting in Maine has such properties. Maybe I'm atop the mother lode of philosopher's stones. I know this: my abilities to be and not to be are heightened here. This mass of hard, compact minerals on which I sit is tailor-made for a straggler, tarry-er, and rolling stoner like me. My decision to move to rural Maine marked the onset of my life as an adult; I garnered work as a junior high school literacy teacher at a six-room schoolhouse in a village about 30 minutes from where I lived and worked in the evenings and weekends as a part-time newspaper reporter for the *Bridgton News*. This decision on my part to launch my adult life in rural New England was no retreat from the world and its mortal concerns. I didn't realize, though, that it would reacquaint me with my *daimon*. I went north to Maine right after graduating from college. It was the first time I had an option about which direction to take. All my childhood and youth, I had little choice but to go due south with my family—from Newport News, Virginia, to Tampa, Florida. Going north was an act of rebellion on my part.

I came to discover and get to know my stone about a week after arriving in Maine. I happened upon it during a meandering drive. I glimpsed the stone as I passed by in my olive green 1974 Ford Pinto with more than 160,000 miles on its odometer. Along one of the less flashy lakes, the stone beckoned. I did a double take, braked, shifted my car into reverse, then parked it on the narrow bed of gravel alongside it.

I hopped atop the flat expanse and surveyed my surroundings. I sat down. I caressed the stone. I wrote down in my journal how it felt, slightly warm to the touch, somehow a bit soft, welcoming. I basked in its company. In that silence and beauty, at some point a voice found me—a voice I recognized but hadn't much been in touch with since my childhood days when I went out alone on the family boat in the Warwick River. Socrates would have called the voice my *daimon*.

In the *Apology*, Socrates characterizes his *daimon* as the voice that tells him not what to do, but what *not* to do:

> You have often heard me speak of an oracle or sign which comes to me, and is the divinity. . . . This sign I have had ever since I was a child. The sign is a voice which comes to me and always forbids me to do something which I am going to do, but never commands me to do anything.

With one exception, I have also found that to be the case when it comes to my own *daimon*. It reappears, or reemerges, almost every time I have returned to the stone over the decades.

As a public school reading teacher at a six-room schoolhouse in the Lakes Region, I had between thirty-five and thirty-seven students per class—seven classes total per day—all of disparate learning abilities, many with difficult if not horrendous family lives. The most meaningful activity I cooked up for them was our weekly Socratic inquiries. I hit upon this in part out of desperation, in part inspiration. Our inquiries had them all leaning in. Underperformers in traditional classroom assignments at last had a chance to shine with their unmatched rhetorical flourishes, to the point that all my students felt over time more like members of a learning community of equals, no matter what assignment they were taking on. They became more inspired to develop their more formal learning arsenal—in my class and other classes of theirs—of reading, writing, drawing, social sciences, hard sciences, history, you name it. They realized on their own that becoming more steeped in such disciplines made them more adept at making impressive contributions to our Socratic inquiries. Best of all, they were sculpting that all-important "fourth R"—reasoning.

Near the close of the academic year, at the end of a school day, one of my students lingered in class. We'd had a Socratic discourse that afternoon on the question "When should you tell a secret?," a question that sprang from their reading of a chapter of a novel that treated that theme. My student, Melinda, or Mindy as she liked to be called, all of twelve years old, told me that she wondered if she should share a secret—one she was instructed not to reveal under any circumstances. She said that the only two people with whom she might feel comfortable sharing it were me and a colleague of mine, a woman who had been teaching at the school for more than two decades and who'd become a close friend and colleague. "Would you tell someone else if I tell you?" she asked, anxious. "I don't know," I replied. "It depends on what you tell me." She thought about this, and left the room. A short while later, my colleague came to see me. Melinda had gone across the hall from my room to hers to share the secret. My colleague and I contacted social services at once.

There was no remotely just or fair ending. The stepfather was arrested, but Mindy's mother blamed her for "telling." She went so far as to accuse her daughter of destroying the family. Melinda was placed in a foster home.

I eventually returned to Virginia after my father had his first open heart surgery, and I went on to become a journalist for a number of noted national magazines; my forte was writing about "unsung heroes," people who on their patch of the earth dedicated themselves to making conditions more fertile and promising for those who lived in bleak circumstances. Mindy and I remained in touch, and my former colleague kept me abreast of what was happening in her life. At age fifteen, Mindy moved to the city of Portland, Maine, where she stayed at a shelter and worked toward completing her high school studies. When I returned to Maine, I sometimes found her with a rough crowd. On one occasion, it took me two days of searching to find her. When I did, she seemed inordinately grateful, even relieved, that I had done so. I took Mindy, then sixteen, to my stone. This was only the second occasion that I ever willfully had company there.

Mindy didn't say a word upon arriving at the stone that day. She sat quietly there with me. Soon, she began taking in deep breaths, and just being. Eventually, she told me that her goal, more than ever, was to be a nurse. "I want to help others heal. But I seem to stand in my own way from succeeding." Then and there, we plotted a path for her to realize her dream and overcome all hurdles, psychological and practical. Her last two years in school, Mindy earned excellent grades even in accelerated science classes. She was then accepted at a nursing school program in Portland. She was on her way.

I managed to find a way to return to Maine at least once a year, to see Melinda and lend her all the support I could, and also visit my stone. Each time I journeyed to the stone, it served as a marker of sorts for me, a lens into my character, my nature, where I was at in life. And, almost invariably, my *daimon* returned.

My unchanging stone brings to mind the visits to the Museum of Natural History by Holden Caulfield of J. D. Salinger's *Catcher in the Rye*. Time and again, Holden returns to his favorite exhibits, like the one with Eskimos fishing and birds flying, frozen in time, always in the same movements. Each visit, he finds the exhibit pieces themselves as unaltered as I do my stone. As Holden puts it,

> The best thing, though, in that museum was that everything always stayed right where it was. Nobody'd move. [. . .] Nobody'd be different. The only thing that would be different would be you.

What is most poignant and disturbing, for me, about this latest visit to the museum that Holden recounts was that when he got to the door, unlike all previous visits, he didn't enter: "[A] funny thing happened. When I got to the museum, all of a sudden I wouldn't have gone inside for a million bucks."

After our latest rendezvous, upon my return to Virginia, I received frequent letters from Mindy. Her latest was mostly upbeat, but at the end she related that her boyfriend of two years—her first committed relationship, she'd said in a previous correspondence—had broken up with her. She wrote, almost in an offhand way, that he broke her heart but that she would figure out a way to bounce back. This was the first week in October 1993. The following week, Melinda repeatedly tried one night to reach me by phone. There were no cell phones in those days. When I arrived home that evening after a late night of work at the newspaper office, my caller ID showed that she'd tried more than twenty times to reach me. I pressed the button to listen. Each and every time, there was a second or two of silence, and then a click as she hung up. I called her throughout the night. At about 4:00 a.m., I received a call from my friend and colleague from years back. Melinda was dead. Drug overdose.

Seven others besides me attended her funeral. I only knew my former colleague. All were distraught; they'd loved her dearly. Like me, they asked themselves what they could have done. None of them had realized that Melinda had reached such a depth of despair in her life after her boyfriend broke up with her. I did not share that Melinda had tried to no avail to reach me the night she took her life. It was more than I could bear. The following day, after mourning at her grave, I ventured to the stone. When I got there, I drove right past it. I didn't even put on the brakes of my rental car. At the time, I wouldn't have gotten out of the car and climbed onto that stone for a million bucks. I was in too agitated a state, not in the disposition to be receptive to its gifts.

I returned again the following fall. This time, I was more receptive. At the stone, I pulled out my journal from all those years ago. It still had blank pages. I wrote out a new life plan. For the first and only time, my *daimon* told me precisely what to do. Melinda's suicide exploded self-imposed obstacles about what I might do with my time remaining on this earth. I'd strayed from my aspiration to live like Socrates. Three years to the day of Melinda's death, on October 9, 1996, after some experimental fits and starts at other locales, I inaugurated a weekly Socrates Café at a coffeehouse in Montclair, New Jersey.

Now, nearly four decades since my first encounter with the stone, I am back. Several years have passed, the longest stretch ever between visits. About ten minutes after I arrive and settle in at my stone, I find—or better put, feel—at my side the only two people who'd ever accompanied me here, Mindy and my dad. The one occasion Dad visited me during my years living and working in Maine, I had brought him here. I was pleased he'd made the effort to come see me, but there was tension, at least on my part. I sensed that he viewed my time living and working in Maine as just an interlude in my professional life. I was his great Greek hope. I didn't know how to begin to justify to him the decisions I was making at that time. I told him about the Socratic inquiries I was having in my classes. He managed a smile—was it my imagination that it seemed forced, masking hidden disappointment? Then he said something surprising: "Keep going your own way in life, Philip." Dad was the only one who on occasion called me Philip, the name of his father and my first name. "I never did that. I couldn't stand up to my mother. I wanted to own a grocery store–café. When I told your *yaya* of my dream, her reaction wasn't . . . pleasant. I did what she directed me to do professionally. Whatever she told me to do was law. I love my work as an engineer and executive, absolutely love it now, don't get me wrong; but it's not what I would have chosen. You keep going your own way, and don't look back." Then and there, my relationship with my father changed. We still had sharp differences on occasion, but more as equals who loved and at times even revered one another.

A boy appears. "I live up the road a piece," he says. If I'm not mistaken, he seems first to speak to my conjured images of Dad and Mindy before they take their leave and vanish into the unknown. He is clutching a fly rod and has several fly lures in his fishing vest. He's also toting a pail with some water in it, presumably for any fish he might catch.

He leaps right onto my stone. "Mind if I do some fly-fishing here? This is my favorite spot."

The kid parks himself on the other side, polite to a fault, giving me my space even as I begrudge his presence. "You want to be alone," he says. "I'm invading your space. But you could use some company—hell, I could too—even if we don't talk. My mom says you shouldn't be alone when you're upset."

Is he talking about me or himself?

He can tell by my reaction that he sees into and through me. "My mom says I'm an indigo child." Indigo children are said to be more attuned to the sufferings of others, freethinkers with astonishing insight into others, spiritually gifted souls.

I smile. "That's how my wife describes our youngest daughter. She also calls her an old soul, says she reminds her of a child we knew in a place called Chiapas, Mexico—someone I just saw for the first time in years, as a matter of fact, not long ago. Not a child anymore. She has a baby of her own."

I'm surprised to find that I am glad of his company. He sets about fishing from a squat position on the other side of the rock. He flicks out his fly rod line again and again, extending it further out into the lake. At times his line zips just a few inches above my head, but he does so with such expertise that I feel no fear. Finally the line settles into the lake just where he wants it, in a shady spot about twenty yards away. "That's where the trout are," he says with confidence.

He makes small talk from time to time. He tells me his mom and dad own a local motel. He says that though all of them were born and raised right in this area, some locals don't treat them so nicely, because their family is originally from Lebanon and their skin is darker than most. I tell him that the family of George Mitchell, former U.S. senator from Maine whom I once interviewed when I was a reporter here, is from Lebanon, and that he should be proud of his heritage.

He thinks about that. He smiles. He continues to fish. The whooshing sound of the line, as he directs it again and again to just the right spot, is pleasant.

Then, he catches a fish. A brook trout at least fourteen inches long.

"That's one of the biggest I've caught here," he says. "But my brother would have said, 'You should've seen the one that got away.' He always said that. Thought it was the funniest thing."

"Would have said?"

"Dylan died five years ago. Head-on car accident. The driver coming in the opposite direction was drunk."

"I'm so sorry."

"He was just sixteen. He'd gotten his driver's license only a month before."

Then he tells me, "The drunk driver was found guilty of manslaughter. Sentenced to ten years in prison. My mother decided after about six months had passed since his sentencing that she wanted to meet him. His name's Sam. He was twenty-one at the time, just about to graduate from college before his sentencing. She got permission to go. Sam also had to agree to it. Mom felt she had to meet the guy who killed her son. Dad didn't stop her from going, but wouldn't go along.

"When Mom met Sam at the prison, he couldn't look her in the face at first. He told her she had every right to confront him. He was afraid she'd scream at him, maybe try to hit him. He felt she had every right. She told him she just wanted to meet him and try to understand how he could do such a thing, be so irresponsible.

"Mom said he cried, begged her for forgiveness. Sam told her both his parents practically disowned him for what he did. These are small towns and everyone knows about it. He said he'd been working two jobs while going to college, and that that night, after he got off work, he'd gone to have a few with friends. A belated celebration of his birthday. He knew he should never have gotten behind the wheel. When he came to after the accident, his car wrapped around a tree, he didn't even know what had happened. He hardly had a scratch.

"Sam didn't want to be let out early from prison. He said he deserved his sentence and more. His life will never be the same, but at least his goes on. Mom began to visit him pretty regularly. After about a year and a half, she helped his attorney file documents supporting his early release. Mom doesn't want to see another young life destroyed, no matter how much pain she and me and Dad are experiencing. Sam's finished his bachelor's degree, and now he's going to graduate school. He's going to be a mental health counselor. He and Mom still get together. I guess you could say they're friends."

He puts down his fishing rod, looking downward into the lake. "My parents had had an argument with Dylan before he went out that night he was killed. I play that scene over and over in my mind. My dad told Dylan he was an ungrateful child. 'You owe us,' he said to Dylan. 'We don't owe you.' Those words exactly. I sat there at the dining table. Didn't say or do anything. Not my battle. As he was leaving the house, Dylan turned around and looked at me in a way he never had before. It was like he knew he'd never see me again. Dylan lifted up his hand, but in an odd way. I couldn't tell if he meant for me to come to him or if he was saying goodbye. Or both. When I didn't respond right away, he turned around and left. We got the call from the police about 1:00 a.m.

"Five years ago now. Dylan would be twenty-one today. Graduating from college. Ready to take on the world.

"I try to be like Mom," he then says. "Full of forgiveness. Some days are harder to do that than others. I live for Dylan now. He was training to be a smoke jumper. It was his end-all, be-all in life. I'll have my certification soon and will be a specially trained wildland firefighter."

After a silent spell, he says, "Dad and I went with Mom the day Sam was released from prison. We felt it was time to meet him. But Dad didn't get out of the car after we arrived. He started bawling. First time I'd ever seen him cry. He said he still hadn't forgiven himself that his final words to Dylan were so harsh. We all hugged and cried."

"I can't even begin to tell you how sorry I am," I say, my eyes welling with tears.

"I go to Dylan's grave every day. Never miss a day, not even in the worst weather. I've heard about 'older brothers from hell,' but Dylan wasn't one of them at all. I mean, we had some fights, we're boys, but nothing serious. I could tell Dylan anything. I told him about my first girlfriend. Told him about our breaking up. Poured out my heart to him. He just listened, sometimes with his arm around me. Helped me get over it."

"I would have given anything to have an older brother like that," I say, moved by what he shared.

He doesn't resume fishing. He throws the fish he caught back into the water and gets up. "I'm going to leave you here now so you can have this place to yourself. I'm going to Dylan's grave, tell him about my fish, imagine I hear him say, 'You should've seen the one that got away.' Thanks for sharing your space."

My space. He comes to this stone all the time, I visit it hardly at all anymore, and he thanks me for sharing it.

"I'm sorry for your own loss," he says as he hops off the stone. "For your loss*es*, I should say. I can tell you don't want to talk about it."

After he's gone, I realize he'd never told me his name, and I'd never asked.

DEATH BE NOT PROUD

Since my father's death, I've gotten to know others who've experienced the most excruciating losses. A humanities professor who'd arranged for me to speak on her campus shared over dinner that her younger sibling, who had Asperger's—she described him as "innocent as a lamb and unconditionally loving"—who lived independently was conned by a couple with a criminal record into a friendship so they could enter his life, gain access to his home, and steal all his assets. After taking everything, they killed him in a grisly way, to make sure he couldn't reveal anything to the authorities. They're now in prison serving life terms without parole. "Those sick people clearly enjoyed the sport of killing him," she said. My driver for my events at a college in the Midwest and with whom I'd developed a rapport told me on our drive back to the airport after I'd completed my commitments that his son, who'd moved to the East Coast, was driving one evening through the city in which he resided when his car broke down. It had seemed lucky when his son was able to make it to a car repair garage that was still open, though it was evening. Then a man who had just robbed, while brandishing a knife, a convenience store a half block away saw the light on at the car repair garage; he inexplicably crossed the street, entered, and repeatedly stabbed his son, killing him. His murderer is awaiting trial. A retired air force colonel who'd invited me to hold a Socrates Café at his church shared with me that he lost his only son, "the shining light of my life," who was following his career path in the military; his son died in a freak parasailing accident while visiting on a break from his intensive studies.

In all my years of travels before my father's death, I can hardly recall anyone sharing such grievous loss with me, though surely I encountered many who had heartrending crosses to bear. I'm sure it says a great deal about me and my own insensitivity at the time. Surely others don't share such things unless convinced the person they're talking to is receptive and understanding. Though as a rule I'm a very private person, these days I also sometimes share my own continued anguish. Yet on this occasion, with the indigo child, I didn't say a word. Even so, he still knew. The pain in my expression and demeanor must be far more evident than I realize, and in the few words that I do share.

DAIMON

In Plato's *Phaedrus*, a discourse on love and rhetoric and reincarnation, Socrates is set to take his leave from his interlocutors. But then, his *daimon* intervenes: "when I was about to cross the river, my divine and accustomed sign happened, and I seemed to hear some voice right there, which didn't let me depart." His *daimon* bidding him not to leave, Socrates returns to the discourse and throws himself back into it, effectively starting it afresh—and this leads all immersed in it to a host of new insights.

Socrates was known to linger in a place, and in place. Without prior notice, he'd stray from his companions, and then become transfixed, unmoving. Take this account in the *Symposium*: Socrates falls behind his friends. They don't notice he's gone until they arrive at the house of Agathon, who will be hosting their drinking party. Agathon sends out a servant to look for Socrates. The servant returns and reports that he came across Socrates "standing still on a neighbor's porch." He says he "had called to Socrates several times, but he didn't stir." Agathon, who does not know Socrates well, characterizes this behavior as odd. But another on hand demurs, and says: "This is a custom of his: sometimes he stands apart wherever he happens to be." Alcibiades—who may not know himself very well, but knows the old philosopher through and through—backs this up. Once, he says, after a particularly perplexing and exhilarating inquiry, "Socrates, having conceived of a problem, stood there on the spot thinking it over from dawn onwards . . . and he didn't let go but stood there searching it out." Alcibiades says Socrates remained that way until daybreak the following day, and when he came to, he said his prayers to the gods and went about his normal day. Agathon is won over by their accounts; he no longer considers Socrates's behavior odd in a pejorative way. "Leave him alone," Aristodemus says. Agathon agrees: "Let him be." When Socrates shows up at last for the drinking party and discourse that night, everyone there, including him, "offered libations and sang a hymn to the gods." Then they have one of the most memorable philosophical give-and-takes ever recorded. Surely that stretch of stillness outside of what we take for time and space was just the refresher he needed in order for that to happen.

It's disappointing that such a respected historian of antiquity like Bettany Hughes would make the pat, and wholly unsubstantiated, assertion that Socrates, in these moments of stone-like stillness, "suffered from some form of epilepsy or 'petit mal' (hence his curious cataleptic seizures when he stared into the distance for hours on end), which in a pious age was interpreted as a malign 'inner voice.'" Socrates had no such thing, and there is not the slightest triangulating evidence to support that. Rather, as he himself says astutely, he was up against "the madness of the multitude" with "nothing . . . sound or right in any present politics."

Socrates's own close companions, to their lasting credit, didn't see him remotely in the light that Bettany Hughes does, and they'd know best; they were there, after all. Hughes would be well served to heed what Socrates's companion tells the rest of their friends after returning from his rendezvous with the unmoving philosopher: "Don't disturb him. Let him be." And for heaven's sake, don't judge him or label him in ways that say more about you and your prejudices and misconceptions than him.

When Socrates's voice genie comes out of the figurative bottle on such occasions, it is no more "malign" than the age in which he lived was pious. *His* voice was pious, and the age in which he lived was malign. Socrates the aberrant one? The one who sought to tear down the walls constructed by those who engage in patronizing, demonizing judgmentalism and "labelism" for pernicious ends? Give me (and more to the point, him) a break. [1] Not only that, if you want to point to where the real pathology was taking hold back then, then you should direct your labeling finger at nearly everyone else in his society except for him.

Socrates dared to stand still when the spirit moved him, whether alone or with a crowd. His friends didn't mind, and it wouldn't have occurred to them to judge him. It was normal for him. Let him be. They surely would've felt the same way if he'd done the opposite and taken off in a run. In his preference for stillness, Socrates stands apart from other famous ancient Greek philosophers, who favored walking as a mode for philosophizing. Raphael's *The School of Athens* features Plato and Aristotle walking in lockstep, pondering a philosophical puzzler. Aristotle's followers were called the Peripatetics, which literally means "those walking about." Aristotle himself was famous for walking along with his students while they philosophized together along the Lyceum's public walk. While the likes of philosophers from Aristotle to Kant were renowned for the clocklike regularity of their walks, Socrates was wholly unpredictable when it came to his bouts of stillness. He could all of a sudden revert to such a state at the most unexpected moments, even while engaged in deep discourse with fellow interlocutors. I, too, have experienced moments of such rapture at Socrates Café. In the heat and at the heart of such inquiry, I straddle worlds, in myriad places at once, my outward stillness precipitated by the most intense and hypnotic inner motion.

Besides the experience of utter outward stillness that at times prompts unequaled inner motion—at times while alone at my stone, but also on occasion triggered while in the midst of philosophizing at a Socrates Cafe—I've attempted other modes. I've engaged, for instance, in a number of fruitful Socrates Café "Walk and Talks" over the years, more akin to what the Peripatetics would do, though I've honestly never found it as meaningful *for me*. Every person has his or her own process for how best to process, or just "to be," alone and with others.

What I'd like to see is ever more experimentation. I suggest we adults all have a go at skipping, leaping, bounding, trying each out for size; testing whether it makes for better contemplativeness, exhilaration, well-being; or contributes to just plain having fun. Imagine, for instance, on your way to and from work, or while pondering a hypothesis or the results of a scientific experiment, or agonizing over a fateful decision in the Oval Office, or while Socratizing, that you sometimes leap and bound and skip, whenever the spirit moves you—or maybe such a spontaneous, unselfconscious outpouring of exuberance is what prompts your spirit to move you in wondrous ways. There is no clear reason why we shouldn't, no good reason why we should ever have stopped partaking in such delightful forms of motion and movement. There may be great reasons for resuming the practice. Besides enhancing our philosophizing, problem solving, and overall mental well-being, it might do wonders for our physical health, our playfulness, might rekindle our childlike but by no means childish spirit of curiosity, creativity, and wonder.

THE WONDER YEARS

As Socrates tells it, his *daimon* first came to the fore when he was a child, emerging hand in hand with his innate and ever growing sense of wonder. In Plato's *Thaetetus*, after puzzling with the lad of that name over matters of natural change, Thaetetus is moved to say, "By the gods, Socrates, I wonder extraordinarily about such things." To which Socrates replies, "This is the philosophers' passion, to wonder," for there is "no other beginning to philosophy than that."

Philosophy begins in wonder. Socrates was the epitome of one who is wonder filled, perplexed, unsettled, engaging in extraordinary inner activity, a state of rapture that outward motion at times would have disturbed. He was marveling at the novel and unfamiliar, puzzling his way through it, much like a child would, transported outside common hours, losing all track of time and extraneous affairs.

With *that* in mind, let's consider that most oft-quoted, and least understood, utterance of Socrates's, in which he reports that, according to the oracle of Delphi, "I am the wisest man alive, for I know one thing, and that is that I know nothing." What's he saying here? That he knows nothing? That would be the case only if he was being a deprecatingly ironic poser. Socrates's expressed view is that all true philosophizing begins with the epiphany that, just when you think you know something once and for all—the origins of the universe, the nature of humans, where courage comes from, how change happens, what virtue is made of—that a new insight comes to light that casts everything you thought you knew into a new light, or into doubt—in either case turning your world upside down. What prompts such life-altering insights? Relentless inquiries of a Socratic kind with inquisitive, searching others who proffer new perspectives and possibilities. Such epistemological earthquakes that arise as a result compel an honest searcher on a quest for verifiable, hard-won knowledge to begin the search anew—not at the beginning, but anew, with the exciting prospect that a paradigm may be looming. You are *not* armed (or disarmed) with a blank slate, but with a fresh one with new possibilities for knowing, being, doing that are now open for exploration. Socrates believed he didn't know anything once and for all, though he wondered what it would be like to be one of those know-it-all Sophists who were cocksure that they not only knew everything once and for all, but should charge others a pretty penny to dispense their "wisdom."

Consider this instance of Socrates engaging in soaring speculative philosophical flights in Plato's *Phaedo* after a close encounter with his *daimon*:

> There are many marvelous places on earth, and the earth itself is
> neither of the quality or size that's supposed by those who usu-

ally talk about it. It is huge and we inhabit only a small part of it, around and about the sea, like ants or frogs around a pond; and many other beings live elsewhere in many other such places. For there are many hollows of all sorts—both in shape and size— everywhere around the earth, into which water and air and mist flow together.

In Socrates's time, the earth was considered the center of the physical universe, with the rest of it emanating outward to infinity and beyond. In this piece of pondering, he clearly seems to be—in the fifth century BC—anticipating wormholes, as well as other sentient creatures or life forms on other planets, even "hollows" like black holes.

On such occasions, Socrates was in no retreat from mortal concerns, yet he isn't addressing or encountering them in typical space-time either, because he isn't *in* typical space-time in such moments. Imagine the incredible state of intensive mental activity that can only come from within a self-concocted cocoon of stillness and silence; and appreciate the deafening external white noise coming from the surrounding polis, in growing chaos, within which he created this cocoon. He was in the precise opposite state of being of most of his fellow Athenians, who were now wonder-less—who were the antithesis of "the philosophers' passion, to wonder," for there is "no other beginning to philosophy than that," and no other possible redemptive ending than to keep wondering.

LESSONS BEFORE DYING

Friedrich Nietzsche asserts in *The Gay Science*, "The secret for harvesting from existence the greatest fruitfulness and the greatest enjoyment is—*to live dangerously!*" By this he did not mean taking wanton risks, but to give life all you have, and if you can, as Nietzsche writes in *Twilight of the Idols*, "to die proudly when it is no longer possible to live proudly." Nietzsche did not weigh in on the matter how one should die, though presumably a dignified passing was his preference whenever possible.

My dad had no fear of death. He *did* have a fear of dying a certain way. He planned carefully and methodically over the course of decades in order to make sure that he could die proudly, which to him was tantamount to dying with dignity. For him that meant living independently until his last breath, at his home, rather than at a hospice or a nursing home. Dad's one fear, as he said often over the years, was of being confined to a nursing home if and when the time came that he was too frail and infirm to care for himself. Dad saved his pennies like no other person I've ever known, in part in order to ensure that he could have in-home nursing care, perhaps for years, if the situation warranted it, and still have plenty left over as inheritance to others.

Dad never needed in-home care. Apparently, his life ended abruptly. His half century of painstaking savings disappeared, poof. My mother, who was not with Dad at the time (they had been separated for more than a decade), said she began receiving condolence calls before she'd even been told by those with him at the end that he had died. She related to me that she'd been told that Dad died in fear that someone was whisking him away in a van to a nursing home. She said she was horrified that he may have spent his last hours terrified, far removed from the kind of proud death he longed for and deserved.

Socrates had no fear of death in itself, either. He lived a certain way, come what may or may not afterward. He poses this question in *Thaetetus*: "What evidence could be appealed to, supposing we were asked at this very moment whether we are asleep or awake?" The reply from Thaetetus is, "Indeed, Socrates, I do not see by what evidence it is to be proved; for the two conditions correspond in every circumstance like exact counterparts."

Socrates says in the *Apology* that "there is great reason to hope that death is a good; for one of two things":

either death is a state of nothingness and utter unconsciousness, or, as men say, there is a change and migration of the soul from this world to another. Now if you suppose that there is no consciousness, but a sleep like the sleep of him who is undisturbed even by dreams, death will be an unspeakable gain. . . . For eternity is then only a single night. But if death is the journey to another place, and there, as men say, all the dead abide, what good, O my friends and judges, can be greater than this?

Socrates goes on: "What would not a man give to converse with Orpheus and Musaeus and Hesiod and Homer? Nay, if this be true, let me die again and again!" For Socrates, either possibility—eternal unconsciousness, or an eternal locking of hearts and minds with luminaries across the ages and epochs—is ideal in its way. There may be many other possibilities besides the two Socrates came up with. Even if he'd been able to fulfill his wish of dying again and again, he would have wanted to do so proudly each and every time. The important "Socratic lesson," though, is that no matter how or when you die, no matter your beliefs about an afterlife or lack thereof, a life lived a certain way here and now is its own reward. Such was the life he led, and in a way the life my dad led—lives of overcoming setbacks and reversals, of perseverance in the face of daunting obstacles and withering setbacks, without resentment, and in fact with considerable joy.

RADICAL ATTACHMENT

So many of life's misfortunes demand a heartfelt response, one that might include an outpouring of frustration, anger, anguish, as well as love, understanding, and striving, along with more clarity (perhaps following considerable soul-searching) of mission and purpose and direction. Such a response also can show that it's hard to keep a good person down. Some of those who survive staggering defeats and reversals can nonetheless channel them in ways that over time lead to the fashioning of something quite meaningful out of them, in some cases even when they are the result of base acts of evil. I might bear up to certain physical pains in "stoic" fashion, as is my wont—like when I shattered three ribs last year and fractured a wrist and kept a stiff upper lip—and some emotional ones as well, including staggering professional setbacks, of which I have had many, and defeats in some kinds of competitions and such. But overall and all told, I would never sacrifice the passion and joys that are intermixed with deep agony and suffering, no more than would Socrates or prophets like Jeremiah and Ezekiel.

"If you have an enemy, do not requite him evil with good," Friedrich Nietzsche instructs in *Thus Spoke Zarathustra*. "Rather, prove that he did you some good." Better yet, don't consider him an enemy or antagonist in the first place, even if such a person considers you one. If you have a soul of goodness, you have no need to "prove" to yourself or anyone else that such a person did you some good. Sometimes there is no sugarcoating the fact that an evil act has been perpetrated and served no beneficent purpose of any sort. You or others may be forever damaged as a consequence, and understandably so. Even so, out of that you may sculpt something creative and illuminating that might also be of service to others—a play, or a book, or a nonprofit project or professional pursuit, or everyday displays of empathy and understanding to "fellow sufferers" with whom you now have a shared experience and to whom you might otherwise never have reached out. You may also come to the realization that you are not as different as you might like to think you are from those who do the most abominable acts, even if you never do one yourself.

Suffering, setbacks, and growth are entwined. In cultivating the development of a healthy soul, if you can manage to own your suffering, at least for a while, you can steer and channel it in ways that do some considerable good, and that lead to much greater self-understanding—and much less harsh judgment of others, including those who do the worst things, even if and as you try to set to rights certain wrongs.

The "times that try men's souls," as Thomas Paine, the English-born American philosopher, political theorist, and revolutionary rabble-rouser puts it, are those times that test your mettle. They put to the ultimate test whether your deeds are in alignment with your words. More than that, if you seek at all costs to avoid suffering, you evade many of life's most important challenges, and the lessons that come from meeting them. It's not just a matter, as Nietzsche puts it in *Twilight of the Idols*, of embracing the perspective that "what doesn't kill me makes me stronger." Despair, heartbreak, loss don't have to lead as a matter of course to crippling and paralyzing despondency, though sometimes they can, at least for a while, and for good reason. With some prospective "cures," though, you stand to lose far more than you stand to gain.

I cast my lot with Socrates. The life he exemplified of radical attachment and attunement, and the kind of suffering it entails—and the kind of joy, love, forbearance, and forgiveness that can be wrought from that—is the only life for me.

NOTE

1. Poring over the literature about Socrates and his moments of stillness, I note that some modern psychiatrists have proved as prone as historians and academic philosophers and the like to take potshots at him and grossly mischaracterize his behavior as schizophrenia or some other mania. Incredibly, one prominent psychiatrist goes so far as to say that he was having a full-blown psychosis brought on by hyperventilation, reaction and response to certain sounds or visual stimuli, and auditory hallucinations.

THE CANCER WARD

From Portland, Maine, I again traversed the U.S., this time to central California, a short distance inland and a bit northeast of the Big Sur coast. An administrator of a palliative care program at a medical center in the region had arranged for me to hold a Socrates Café. Over a decade ago, she'd taken part in an ongoing gathering established at her college by a professor who'd read my first book and assigned it in her classes. Upon graduation, she launched her own Socrates Café at a coffeehouse in her community. We'd been in touch for some years, and she'd at last gotten approval for me to inaugurate one with the palliative care program's patients.

The Socrates Cafés I've held over the years at hospices and hospitals for children and for adults with life-threatening and terminal illnesses have been incomparably meaningful. Those who take part often are shut off from the rest of the world just when they are most in need of feeling connected—and when, more than ever, we can learn so much from the vast stores of wisdom they have to impart. The question we explored today came at the suggestion of one of the patients: "What are good days?"

After our inquiry in a brightly decorated common room at the hospital came to a close, a woman named Athena lingers. She waits for everyone else to leave before she comes up to me. Just like my father, who'd attended many of my Socrates Cafés across the U.S., Athena didn't say a word during the formal gathering, though she was listening intently. Again like my father, only after the official gathering winds down does she share her thoughts with me, and only with me.

"I wasn't going to attend," Athena says to me. "Sometimes it can be really hard to say, 'I'm going to do something today.' I'm glad I did come, glad I heard all of the thoughtful people. I wanted to support them, cry with them, laugh with them, be there to hug them when they needed one. We're a community of love here."

Then she says, "As I was listening, it occurred to me that you can't know what your philosophy of a good day is until you know your philosophy of bad days. For me, there are no bad days. Only bad moments. Like when I lose my hair, again. Or when I'm in too much pain to lie down, or to get up, on my own. In such moments, I ask, 'Why me?'

"I've never had a bad day, though, not even on the worst days since I was diagnosed last year with stage four ovarian cancer. I'm more aware of every good and bright and beautiful thing. I'm so appreciative of any gesture of kindness towards me, of anyone who shows me some tenderness, or who lets me show some to them, who makes me still feel like I'm needed.

"The bad moments don't require awareness. They just are. They make me more appreciative of all that is good throughout my day. When I'm able to pick up my nephew and endure the pain. When I can light my votive candles without assistance and give thanks for still being alive. When I'm able to fall sleep at night without too much pain. Even when that's not possible, I haven't—not one time—considered any of my days totally 'bad.' They're all good days, wrapped around some moments of bad and sad.

"I've learned so much about love," Athena says next. "And loss. I've been abandoned by some I thought would always be there for me. I've been embraced by some I never thought would do so.

"It was hard for me at first to get past my own suffering and pain. Now I feel others' pain too, no more so than those in this palliative care community, because of our shared experience of terminal cancer. In a single moment, any one of us here can experience anger, pain, suffering, love, joy.

"Before my cancer," Athena says, "a good day for me would have been one in which I'd had an accomplished day at the office. I was a rising star as a civil engineer at my firm. Thirty-two years old, the sky the limit. That good day was usually rounded off pleasantly: my fiancé and I would meet at our home after work, turn off phones and computers, sit together on our porch, holding hands and sipping wine as we look out over the valley. Nothing like 'being' with the love of your life.

"Almost every Saturday, Kevin and I would make the ninety-minute drive to the Big Sur coast. We'd have a picnic. Watch the sun set. I almost always wore my wet suit. At some point, I'd dive into the ocean and swim about twenty-five yards out to a set of rocks that are so one of a kind they look plopped there from outer space.

"Kevin marveled that I could swim in the Pacific Ocean on even the coldest day. It's something I'd done since I was a child, when my mother and I would do it together. With Kevin watching from shore, I'd swim out to those rocks, then climb to the top and survey the universe."

She shows me a photo of her doing just that. "This wasn't from that long ago—when I was still me and we were still us." I tell Athena that I'm positive I know exactly where this place is, that my wife Ceci and I had once driven there, in the late 1990s. Ceci and I had decided to take a scenic coastal drive south from where we were living in the state's northern Bay Area. Though we still had a long drive ahead of us, it was impossible to pass by those rocks without stopping and taking them in. We parked our car and watched the sun set there, almost precisely twenty years ago. But that's not where the similarity ends. My wife Ceci, just like Athena, is an inveterate cold-water swimmer.

Athena can hardly believe the coincidence. I scarcely can myself.

She says after a while, "Mom came to the U.S. from Colombia when I was two. She was a waitress at a diner. A beloved waitress. Made excellent tips. Saved every penny. Put me through college without taking out a penny in loans. She refused to be in financial debt to anyone. Mom was an incredible soul. She named me Athena, after the Greek goddess of wisdom, and also after Saint Athena, one of the forty Holy Virgins.

"Mom died at age fifty-eight of breast cancer. We had five precious months between the time of her diagnosis and her death. She died knowing how much she was loved, how meaningful a life she had lived, what a powerful example she had set for me. I felt fortunate that we were able to share a loving, lingering goodbye."

I tell Athena that the one thing that is hardest for me to bear is that I wasn't afforded the chance to say my goodbyes to my own father before he died, though it is no small consolation that every single one of Dad's closest friends told me I was for him the source of so much pride and joy—something he'd always found difficult to say directly to me. "Hold on to what they told you," she says, taking my hands and holding them tightly. "What he said about you is a lasting gift."

Eventually, she says to me, "My life changed six months ago. . . . I'd come to this hospital for an exam after experiencing sharp pain in my abdomen. The doctor who broke the news to me—that I had stage four ovarian cancer—was so matter of fact about it. She didn't try to brace or prepare me for what was coming. She just told me, without emotion, then asked if I had health insurance. I wonder how she'd feel if she was talked to like that, told in the coldest, most unfeeling way that life as she knew it was over, and that her life itself would be over in a matter of months.

"I'll never have children," Athena says, her voice breaking. "Never achieve my personal or professional dreams. I was immersed in overseeing a huge public works project that my firm was contracted to do in Colombia. It meant the world to me to do this, knowing how proud Mom would be.

"I've had to go through a journey to accept that I will never be a part of that project again," she says next, "to accept that my own professional life is over. I grieve. I grieve that my fiancé left me. I would still like to have another love, in the time I have left. I want to show and give all my love again to someone.

"I celebrate that a high school friend from whom I'd become estranged has been here for me every step of the way. The political differences we had that led to our estrangement? They're less than nothing. I've learned so much about love, about what really matters. This doesn't make me 'glad' I have cancer, but it has made me a better human being."

Soon afterward, she says, "You'll be back here to hold another Socrates Café in four months. I won't see you again. Thank you for today. Such a good day. Such an excellent day."

A couple of hours later, Athena texts me. "I wish I'd told you to go out again to those rocks on Big Sur."

I text her back, along with a photo: "I'm here now, thinking of you, and of your precious mother."

ATHENA

Less than a month later, Athena died. I carry this beautiful soul with me now. In one of my upcoming trips to Brazil, where my work has become popular, I will also make a side journey to Bogotá, Colombia, to visit the public works project she was integrally involved in implementing as a civil engineer. I will also make my way by bus to her mother's native town of Popayan, in Cauca, and hold a Socrates Café. Athena had asked me to, and put me in touch with those who could help arrange it. She said the inhabitants there were like her and her mother—open; inquisitive; curious and friendly (*calida*); full of passion, drive, and determination even in trying circumstances.

Athena's mother named her daughter appropriately. Myth has it that Greece's most famous and important city, Athens, came to get its name after the Greek goddess Athena was pitted in a contest with Poseidon to perform miraculous feats. Athena won the day with her creation of an olive tree, which signifies health, peace, fertility (even in times of drought), and prosperity. It was considered by the populace that voted for the winner to be of far more value than Poseidon's demonstrations of brute power and strength. At the time, when at their peak as a virtuous society, Athenians placed much more of a premium on what Socrates calls in Plato's *Cratylus*—a discourse largely on the nature and purpose of language—Athena's "divine mind" and "ethical wisdom." Socrates traced his own ethical development as one that was attempting to follow the example and the trajectory—in his case as a mortal—of Athena, the patron goddess of wisdom.

By the time of Socrates's trial, Athenians no longer valued such divine wisdom. Their defeat in the Peloponnesian War was widely viewed by polis denizens as an unmistakable sign that they'd been impious. Remarkably, instead of owning up to the fact that they themselves were the root cause of this impiety, they blamed Socrates. They claimed that his impiousness, not theirs, was the deciding factor in their defeat by the Spartans, because he chose to worship a different pantheon of gods than the ones sanctioned by their oligarchy. This was scapegoating pure and simple, but they preferred anything to the mordant truth, that they only had themselves to blame. You don't accept such blame, and the responsibility that comes with it, when you are part of a pervasive pathology that makes dishonesty and finger pointing the rule rather than the exception.

Socrates *did* go his own way and fashion his own pantheon of gods and goddesses, Athena—of whom he was an ardent worshipper—among them. The divine wisdom she embodied and that he emulated in his own mode of being could only be had from seeking continually to discover more and more about "right conduct." Socrates says in *Cratylus* that he agrees with Homer (who Socrates refers to as "an ancient") that Athena "represents intellect and thought," indeed that she is "divine intelligence." To Socrates as with Homer, Athena "*has* intelligence *about* divine things surpassing that of all others."

After his encounter with the oracle priestess-mystic at Delphi, Socrates's mission for the remainder of his life was to gain the kind of wisdom that can only be had by asking questions that carry one further forward in the pursuit of right conduct. He carried Athena figuratively on his shoulders every step of the way, convinced that one gained the kind of divine wisdom she extolled and modeled through questioning that in effect "removed the mist from the eyes" of an inquirer and hence "discern both God and Man." What does this mean? To discover "the divine within . . . whereby you may distinguish between good and evil."

Wisdom, by this conception, is a process, not an entity, and lies in discovering how best to go about clearing the mist from your eyes so you better can discern good from evil, and practice more adeptly good and right conduct rather than its converse. It also implies that wisdom itself can be of a good or not so good sort—hence the adjective *ethical* wisdom. Wisdom of this kind does *not* mean you judge or label another person as good or evil, regardless of whether that person commits godly or loathsome acts. Rather, as you become more endowed with Athena-like ethical intelligence, you yourself are better able to distinguish those acts that are good from those that aren't, and as a result you'll engage even more faithfully and diligently in right conduct. And, as you yourself stumble and fall short of your ideals, you'll further sculpt the humility needed to understand nonjudgmentally even the extreme failings, fragilities, and foibles of others in your orbit, and to feel their pain (even if you don't forgive altogether) even when they undertake deliberately hurtful and malevolent misdeeds directed at you and those you most love.

THE PATH OF A *NINGEN*

In 2006, I held a Socrates Café at Hiroshima Peace Memorial Park in Japan—an unforgettable exchange that explored participants' philosophies of the Japanese concept of *ikigai*, which translates as "that which makes life worth living." The children who'd been part of that inquiry—which I recount in *Socrates in Love: Philosophy for a Die-Hard Romantic*—had traveled to Hiroshima, where on August 6, 1945, an atomic bomb was dropped by a U.S. military B29 bomber, destroying most of the city and killing approximately 140,000 people. They had come from Kyoto with their middle school class to visit the park and its Peace Memorial Museum situated in the center of the city. They were mostly eleven and twelve years of age at the time. That particular Socrates Café already was underway, and floundering—none of the adult participants said they felt life was much worth living these days—when the young students happened upon us and decided to take part, after seeing my large poster that said in English and Japanese, "Socrates Café: Everyone welcome." Before their arrival, the adults on hand had been declaiming Japanese youth as "valueless" and even "worthless," the veritable scourge of their country's problems, because of their putative lack of appreciation for traditional values. Without being privy to this scathing critique of Japanese youth by the adults on hand, the students shared with us, with passion and conviction, the projects to build world peace that they planned to launch upon returning home. One child, Arisa, said her *ikigai* from here on out would be to do all she could to make sure what happened at Hiroshima and Nagasaki never happened again. To that end, she said, as soon as she returned home to Kyoto, she was going to start an email chain letter campaign that offered a daily prayer for peace and that encouraged people—everywhere, every single day—to take at least one action that would make the world more peaceful. Arisa did just that. Hundreds of thousands, all told, including me, became part of her chain letter project over the years, and we shared our daily efforts to make the world a more understanding and connected one. Arisa and I have stayed in touch on and off over the many years since.

A little more than a year ago, she opened a small bookstore outside of Kyoto with a childhood friend, Yoshio. Each of them is married, each with a young daughter. They agreed at the outset of launching their bookstore that each of them could invite an author from any part of the globe to come to their store as their guest, all expenses paid by them, to hold a book event.

Arisa invited me. From Los Angeles, the flight to Tokyo was approximately ninety-two hundred kilometers, or about fifty-five hundred miles, followed by a two-hour train trip to Kyoto, which once was Japan's capital and is known for its Buddhist temples and gardens and Shinto shrines.

The bookstore of Arisa and Yoshio is about the size of a studio apartment, with soft lights, a carpet in earth tones, and books displayed from floor to ceiling, yet without anything seeming crowded. They've made masterful use of every square inch of interior space, with portable shelves that open and close and tables on wheels that can be rearranged or pushed aside in a jiffy.

An intimate and animated group of about fifteen people seated in folding chairs attend my presentation (Arisa and Yoshio serve as translators) about my Socratic sojourns around the globe that includes a reading by the owners from my *Socrates Café*, published in Japanese. Though everyone on hand did buy a copy of my book, it didn't begin to cover the cost of my travels. Any worries I had afterward that Arisa and Yoshio might have regretted inviting me were quickly dashed by the owners' evident joy and pleasure. By whatever criteria they used to classify the event as a success, this has met it.

The following day, I take Arisa and Yoshio up on their invitation to visit the historic part of Kyoto and walk along *Tetsugaku-no-Michi*, the Philosopher's Path. The meandering footpath is about two kilometers long, with a ribbon of a canal snaking along one side that's part of a vast network powering the country's state-of-the-art (and first-ever) hydroelectric power plant. The path's name stems from the fact that Japan's acclaimed philosopher, Nishido Kitaro (1870–1945), walked and meditated along it nearly every day of his standout career on his way to and from Kyoto University. Much like Socrates, Kitaro could sometimes also be seen in a state of absolute stillness at some point along the trail; presumably he was grappling with complex problems about the nature of reality and man's place in the universe about which he wrote in best-selling books that to this day influence great thinkers and everyday people alike and that reveal hidden likenesses among the world's philosophical and cultural traditions.

The Philosopher's Path is conducive to contemplation—or to not contemplating at all, to emptying your mind. We enter it just north of the Eikan-do Temple. It is not yet cherry blossom season, so the trees filled with buds that line the path aren't yet exploding in a blaze of pink—meaning it is not yet so packed with people as it will be in another week or so. In fact, there are times when we have the Philosopher's Path to ourselves.

My companions share with me that Eikan-do Temple, built in the mid-ninth century, is named after the abbot Eikan, beloved for his outreach to the poor and sick. The abbot had built on the grounds of the temple a hospital to care for the neediest in the region. "Japan is all about gates, which are usually meant to exclude," Yoshio tells me. "For the abbot, though, the gates for entering this temple weren't meant to keep people out, but to let them know it was open to one and all and that they were entering a welcoming and loving place. Effectively, a gateless gate."

This first part of the winding Philosopher's Path along which we walk is bordered by a deep green, wooded hillside. The water rippling over small stones in the canal on the opposite side makes almost a musical sound. The hurly-burly world ceases to exist. We walk mostly in silence at a slow pace for nearly a kilometer, at times pausing at the small shrines. At about the midpoint of the well-trodden path, we ascend an ancillary gravel trail and enter a teahouse also known for its delectable Buddhist vegetarian fare. It affords a sweeping view of the city. The entrance is narrow and low, so we have to bow our heads. Arisa tells me that it is intentionally designed this way, so that guests have no choice but to lower their heads in a bowing motion, as a way of greeting the host of the teahouse.

After we order, I tell Yoshio and Arisa that on my train ride to Kyoto from Tokyo, something odd happened. "When the train crew attendant came to punch my ticket, he looked at it, then started waving it at me. I had no idea what he was saying, but he wasn't happy. Then, a man in casual dress about six rows in front of us got up and beckoned to the attendant. He whispered something to him, then seemed to reach inside his sweater. The attendant became quite calm, gave a slight bow to the man and walked away, not even looking my way again. The passenger gave me a brief glance, maybe a small nod of his head, and sat down. That was that."

Yoshio asks where on the train I was sitting. I tell him I was on the upper level of the train so I could get a good view of all I was passing, and that there was very pleasant individual service. I showed them my punched ticket. "You were in first class, and your ticket was coach," he says. "That man paid the difference in your fare and for your meal." The difference was a princely sum.

Yoshio then puts his hands to his cheeks, his look one of dismay. "I shouldn't have told you. That gentleman would never have wanted you to know what he did."

"I'm glad you did," I say. "I wish I'd known then, so I could have expressed my gratitude, and offered to pay him back."

"That's the last thing he would have wanted," Arisa says. "He was a real and true *ningen*. You see, *he* was the one who felt gratitude, for being able to be of service to you. He wouldn't want you to know what he did, or feel gratitude for his act, precisely because then you might have felt some obligation either to repay him or 'pay it forward.'"

"If you yourself are a real and true *ningen*, you'd do the same kind of thing he did if you saw someone in need or distress," says Yoshio. "He reminds me of that woman in Chiapas you first met when she was a child whom you told us about last night at your presentation. A real and true *ningen* is sort of like a *batsil winic*, a true human being."

"*Ningen* is Japanese for person," Arisa says. "It doesn't mean 'individual.' A person *is* a social being. That's what Aristotle taught, too. It's also what the people believe with whom you held dialogues in Soweto, South Africa. You shared last night that they live by the tribal democratic concept of *ubuntu*, 'I am in you and you are in me.'"

She then says, "The first part of *ningen*—*nin*—means 'human being,' and the second—*gen*—means 'space' or 'in between.' A *ningen* isn't simply an entity, a human entity, but exists between and among the spaces—between and among ourselves and other people, other places, other things, other worlds."

And then: "My husband and I bought a home, after saving up for it for many years. We wanted our baby girl-to-be to be raised in a home of her own. There was all this unsightly kudzu in the front yard, almost like enormous monstrous bushes, invading our yard and the façade of our home, even eating into the bricks. One of our neighbors came by to introduce himself. I asked him if he knew anyone who could remove all the kudzu. He said without hesitation, 'I'll do it.' He did, the next day. It took him the entire day, backbreaking work, and he also transported it in a pickup truck the long distance to where you have to dispose of such things. It took him four long trips, the back of his pickup truck filled each time, to tote it all and dump it there. He refused to accept any payment. 'I'm just being a neighbor,' he said. He didn't say 'good neighbor,' only 'neighbor.'

"I found out later from another neighbor that he had rented a pickup truck to do the transporting part of it. I went to his house and insisted that he allow me to pay for the rental and gas. He was very upset. Almost to the point of distraught. He didn't want my gratitude. 'This is just what we do,' he said. Not 'what I do.' 'What *we* do.'"

"*Ningen* translates as 'interpersonal' or 'interhuman,'" says Yoshio. "You don't exist except in the context of your relations. Whether we realize it or not, we all lean on each other—lean on our fellow humans, lean on society, the universe, and they lean on us. It makes us almost humans without borders.

"You see, you don't become an exceptional teacher or politician or bookstore owner or financial advisor and then become a *ningen* as a result. When you're a *ningen*, no matter your pursuit, you will be exceptional at it, in a way that benefits everyone and everything else."

Then Arisa says, "That man on the train, he doesn't care about your social status. He might also help a rich person who's in need in some way. He makes no distinctions. He'll help whenever he sees an opportunity, without expectation or desire of anything in return. It gave *him* gratitude and satisfaction.

"Acts of a real and true *ningen* are meant to escape notice, in the sense that the person who does them doesn't want to bring attention to himself. All that matters is the deed. Take Chiune Sugihara. He lived as if his own life wasn't worth living unless he was willing to risk his standing, and perhaps even his life, for others whose lives were in jeopardy."

Chiune Sugihara was a Japanese diplomat stationed in Lithuania. In the summer of 1940, he defied the orders of his superiors in Tokyo and issued more than six thousand visas to Lithuanian Jews and Jewish refugees from German- and Soviet-occupied Poland so they could flee Europe. Sugihara was dispatched to Kaunas, Lithuania, in the fall of 1939 to open a consulate. Since no Japanese citizens lived in that country, Sugihara couldn't fathom why he'd been posted there, though at the time Japan was an ally of Nazi Germany, which had invaded the country. In 1940, refugees and others fearing persecution began coming to the gates of his consulate each day, the majority of them Polish Jews seeking a way out of Europe. Sugihara and his family—he lived in a small apartment inside the consulate with his wife and young children, including a newborn—were awakened most mornings by would-be visa seekers clamoring at the gates. His superiors at the Foreign Ministry in Tokyo told him in no uncertain terms that he was forbidden from issuing visas to them.

After learning from intelligence reports what the horrible fate would be if those seeking escape didn't succeed in securing visas, Sugihara defied his bosses' orders. Over the course of two months, barely sleeping, he processed thousands of visas, writing them out by hand. His wife, at his side, would massage his cramped hands so he could keep writing them out and processing them. Because of Sugihara and his wife, thousands of Polish Jews seeking refuge both from the Soviet invaders and Nazi persecution were able to depart, and survive.

"Not even his children learned about his extraordinary deed until they were quite old themselves," Arisa tells me. "It was all there in the official records, but Sugihara never made a single mention of it the rest of his life. To him, his heroism was just 'what we do.'"

In 1984, when Sugihara's heroic effort finally came to light, he was named by Yad Vashem—Israel's official memorial to victims of the Holocaust—"righteous among the nations," a title bestowed on non-Jews who risked their lives to rescue Jews from the Holocaust. "One book I read about him described him as 'a true *mensch*,' Yiddish for a person of honor and integrity," says Yoshio. "I'm sure Sugihara would have shrugged off the accolade and said simply, 'I'm a *ningen*.' Meaning: any other *ningen* encountering such a situation, in which a group of human beings is persecuted and treated in an inhumane way, would have done the same thing. Sugihara was bearing witness—not just by learning the nightmarish true facts of what was really taking place, but by how he acted upon what he learned. He felt it his duty and responsibility. But he wouldn't have put it in those explicit terms, because to him that went without saying."

There is a long interval of comfortable silence. Eventually Yoshio says, "People aren't 'atomistic' by the *ningen* concept. They're made up of all the countless relations and connections they forge and foster as they interact with the universe. A *ningen* values the intervals of space, the 'in-betweens'—like the space between beginnings and endings, life and death."

To which Arisa says, "The pauses and silences—the pause in speech that conveys so much meaning, or the silence between the notes that make the music. That space between musical notes, those silences, give form to the whole of what's being said or composed or performed.

"The Japanese concept of *ma* means the space or gap or interval between spatial or temporal things or events—but one that connects rather than separates them. It's similar to the silence experienced between notes of a melody."

Yoshio then says, "It also can mean 'opening.' We have a term—*mono ko ma*. Mono means 'thing.' When you combine the terms *mono* and *ma*, it signifies 'the opening between things'—and by things, it isn't just meant by that to be objects, but also people, events, feelings, time itself."

"Or," says Arisa, "it can be that space or interval between the familiar and the strange, or between something and nothing, or between what can be described and what can't be put into words, even between memory and loss."

This gives me considerable pause. "So it can even be between life and death. Not so much a passageway or transition, but a connector." I go on to tell them that this brings to mind that beautiful passage in Thornton Wilder's Pulitzer Prize–winning *The Bridge of San Luis Rey*, one that I've read many times since my father's passing:

> But the love will have been enough; all those impulses of love return to the love that made them. Even memory is not necessary for love. There is a land of the living and a land of the dead and the bridge is love, the only survival, the only meaning.

And then I tell them, "I'm not sure such a bridge between the two lands is, as a matter of course, love itself. It's up to us to construct it out of the materials of love. Or the bridge collapses."

By the time we leave the tearoom, it is late in the day. Fireflies are starting to make an appearance on the Philosopher's Path that we've resumed walking. "Every time I walk here, I feel close to Nishida Kitaro," says Yoshio. "This path came to be out of the thousands of times he walked the same trail over many decades."

Over the years, I have read a great deal about and by Kitaro, who not only also absorbed Western philosophy, starting with the ancient Greeks, but managed to integrate the best of that heritage with

Eastern philosophy, Japanese philosophy in particular. In an era in which his own country was swept up in nationalistic fervor, he set out to show how beautifully equal we are.

One of his protégés, Nishitani Keiji, writes this about Kitaro, saying that whenever he philosophized,

> the words flowed out of him as if charged with electricity and occasionally erupted into flashes of lightning. . . . To me it felt like listening to a great piece of music—at times feeling struck by something in my innermost being, at times wafted into flight as on the wings of a bird. His lectures truly touched the spirit.

Kitaro continued being a *ningen* in a time of national madness, even as he experienced tragedy in his private life: his wife died after a protracted illness, and four of his eight children died young, three of them from typhus. As he walked the Philosopher's Path, it is said that the magnificent pine and cherry blossom trees, along with the ancient temples and shrines, gave him solace. While he was often seen walking on campus in animated conversations with students and colleagues, when on the Philosopher's Path, he walked alone; it was a retreat that helped him cope with the excruciating loss of several he loved most. It also intellectually inspired him, leading him to new philosophical pathways to consider, always starting from what he called pure or direct experience, and working its way outward.

As we arrive at the south end of the Philosopher's Path, we come to a stone that commemorates Nishida Kitaro. "He also wrote short *waka* poetry," Arisa says. "He wrote one after the passing of his first son. Part of it goes: 'How could he disappear like a dream.' And another, about the loss of so many in his family, goes in part: 'The bottom of my soul has such depth; neither joy nor the waves of sorrow can reach it.'"

Arisa looks at me. "Your soul itself is made of waves of joy and sorrow. It doesn't have a top or bottom, surface or depth. It's the space in between, the *ma*. To reach it—this place and space—you have to find the gateless gate inside. You had told me in one email before you traveled to Japan about your beloved father's passing. If you find this gateless gate, your father will be there to welcome you and open it for you."

THE IN-BETWEEN WORLD

On the return train trip to Tokyo from Kyoto, I consider further this profound concept of *ma*. Nearly all my exchanges with those I've had the great good fortune to encounter, whether intentionally or serendipitously (or both), during these intensive travels have, à la the Socrates depicted in Xenophon's works, occurred in intervals, pauses—in the spaces between the formal and informal, the intentional and the unexpected. They have been of immeasurable benefit in helping me gain a far keener understanding of how better to deal with the most egregious and grievous kinds of loss and sorrow. Indeed, the conversations themselves, the "process" of having heartfelt interactions with deeply caring people, have been the best salve of all.

I'm further led to wonder whether, in this era marked and marred by extreme polarization, racism, violence, hatred, and resultant acts of evil that stem from this—all this in the midst of an unfolding pandemic of a virulence unlike any experienced in the last century—if the willful creation of a loving *ma* can serve as that space that makes far more likely redemptive forms of human encounter. Can it be that bridge that supplants the chasms we've constructed between those we view as one of "us" and those we look at as "them" or, worse, "the other." Must the bridge be made of love?

In *Rendezvous with the Sensuous: Readings on Aesthetics*, scholar Linda Ardito notes there that after Socrates comes out of one of his stock-still contemplative states, he and his friends offer up a toast to the gods and revel in music:

> It is noteworthy that music underscores the importance of this moment [in the *Symposium*] . . . contrasted and punctuated by the preceding . . . scene of Socrates in a transfixed and silent state on a nearby porch. . . . Here Plato leaves artistically an acoustic space to suggest the stillness conducive of deep, meditative thought.

What is left unplayed, left unsaid, in such acoustic spaces—not a void yet not altogether a threshold or a bridge, but an entity unto itself—is every bit as integral, while the acoustic space she describes is clearly central to how great thinkers like Socrates and Nishida Kitaro contemplate.

OFF THE BEATEN TRACK

The pre-Socratic philosopher Parmenides, one of the most consequential philosophers before Socrates, was founder of the Eleatic school of philosophy, named after the Greek coastal city of Elea, where he lived. His one extant piece of writing, 150 lines from the prologue of his prose poem *On Nature*, seeks to reconcile the unity of nature with its infinite variety.

As Parmenides tells it, he is taken by carriage to the gate that lies between the ways of day and the ways of night. He is held up at the gate in a pettifogging manner by Lady Justice, who holds the keys and decides who can pass through. Parmenides's maidens persuade her to open up the huge gates, and they swing open. After passing through, Parmenides makes his way to the goddess Persephone, who "received me kindly. Taking in her hand my right hand she spoke and addressed me with these words":

> Young man . . . it was no ill fate that persuaded you to travel this way. For no evil fate would set you to travel on this road, far from that taken by mortal men, and beyond their beaten paths; No, it is Rightness and Justice that bring you here to learn all things—both the unshakable heart of well-rounded truth and the opinions of mortals.

If you want to arrive at sound insights, if you want to "see the light" rather than remain mired in darkness, then you must have the proper starting place to do so. The German existentialist philosopher Martin Heidegger was smitten with the pre-Socratics, particularly Parmenides and his pursuit of the essence of being—what Heidegger called "the path of Being." One of the last works of Heidegger's to be published is titled *Off the Beaten Track*. Heidegger had a home on the edge of the Black Forest and often walked along a *holzweg*, or timber track, in a nearby forest that led to a clearing. Heidegger suggests that most moderns have lost their way, with little earthly idea how to find the kinds of *holzweg* from which to embark on journeys that lead to a clearing where there is *lichtung*, a place of light and open space where you "see" in new and different lights.

An inveterate trail walker, Heidegger, like Nishida Kitaro, found that regularly walking along the same familiar path—one that affords unequaled solitude—can put you in just that contemplative state that can lead you to exhilaratingly mystifying, wholly unfamiliar destinations—to new ways and truths and lights (revealed, in his case, in unfortunately opaque if not impenetrable prose). Heidegger thought nonstop about time. He came to the view that it is not of the linear variety, with a clear-cut triad of past, present, and future, and so tenses are not offset by some sort of eternity. Rather, he held, humans themselves *are* time. This jibes with the perspective of Jorge Luis Borges, who writes in *Labyrinths*:

Time is the substance I am made of. Time is a river which
sweeps me along, but I am the river; it is a tiger which destroys
me, but I am the tiger; it is a fire which consumes me, but I am
the fire. The world, unfortunately, is real; I, unfortunately, am
Borges.

BEARING WITNESS

In 1967, my family moved from Newport News, Virginia—the
only placed I'd ever known, besides our months-long summer sojourns to Tampa—to cosmopolitan northern Virginia, on the outskirts of our nation's capital. The move was a must in order for my
ambitious father to work his way up the bureaucratic ladder and
labyrinth that is the Department of Defense. These were my forma-
tive years, not just for the run-of-the-mill developmental reasons,
but even more so because of all that was happening on the civic and
political scene, nowhere more so than in the greater Washington,
D.C., area. While there, I passed through the fourth, fifth, and sixth
grades; fell in love for the first time (Sarah Miller, where are you
now?); and I experienced, thanks to my dad, what would turn out to
be an indelible call to conscience and service.

While we lived in the D.C. area, in the bedroom community of
Arlington, Virginia, on several occasions my father would an-
nounce to my mother, "Chris and I are going for a ride." I would
jump up from whatever I was doing, raring to go. My mother would
bite her lip in evident but tacit concern. She knew what was what.
One of these instances was in April 1968. Dad and I drove off in
our maroon Oldsmobile Dynamic '88, which he'd bought used at a
bargain-basement price, and made our way from our tranquil home
in the pleasant suburbs of Arlington toward the southeast section of
Washington, D.C. Though just six miles away, it was worlds removed. In this deeply segregated part of the city, less than a week
earlier, riots had broken out in the immediate aftermath of the as-

sassination of Dr. Martin Luther King Jr. The civil unrest continued for four tension-filled days—in which over 1,100 buildings were damaged or destroyed, more than 1,000 people were arrested, and over 6,100 injured—and had only ended shortly before Dad made a beeline for the D.C. corridor that had borne the brunt of the mass upwelling of rage against the machine that allowed vast inequities. When we arrived, Dad drove slowly around. In silence we drove along street blocks with broken storefronts, some buildings still smoldering with smoke.

Locals clustered on street corners looked at us in disbelief. One person was close enough for me to hear him say, "What are those white-ass honkies doing?" They let us through safely, maybe in part because, on closer inspection, they saw that the skin of the driver beside me in the bright white pressed shirt was swarthy. I don't know. I know this: Dad himself had been the victim of virulent racism. The son of dirt-poor Greeks, tormented at school by white students because he had a discernible accent, had grown up in a segregated housing project in Florida. He knew firsthand what it was like to have two strikes against you before you were even out of the starting gate of this thing called life.

My dad and I didn't exchange a word as we traversed the area. It wasn't enough for Dad to see such happenings on the news, at a safe distance. We did not gawk. We absorbed. We bore witness.

Two months later, the beginning of June, Dad again told Mom he was taking me for a drive, this time to the Lincoln Memorial. I was bemused, since he often said how much he disliked visiting the typical D.C. tourist attractions ("Once is enough" was his familiar refrain). What I didn't know, as we drove off from home, was that, starting in mid-May, an encampment called Resurrection City had been set up that ran from the National Mall, near the Reflecting Pool, to the Lincoln Memorial (where there is now a World War II Memorial). Thousands of desperately needy families—white, black, Native American, Latino—along with antipoverty activists advocating on their behalf, had converged here from around the country. They set up tents for an encampment, but that was just the half of it. They created a makeshift, fully functioning town, including a mess hall, a school, and a day care center, that at its peak had more than twenty-seven hundred residents. The aim of their Poor People's Campaign was to draw attention to the grave and ever-increasing inequalities in America.

My dad wanted to see it for himself, and he wanted me to see it for myself. Dad knew what it was to grow up in poverty (and in his case without a father after age seven), and the steep odds of escaping it. The unspoken query from Dad to me was: How can you fully feel the pain and plight of the dispossessed and disenfranchised unless you see up close and personal the crosses they have to bear day in and out? I will never forget an encounter with a young African American woman while there. She had four children in tow. Two babies in her arms who looked to be identical twins, a little girl climbing her back, another pulling at her skirt, determined to play with her. While all her children vied for her attention, she came up to me. "Hold my baby, please." I held her baby. She screamed at first. I started making cooing sounds, and jiggled her, then brought her close to my shoulder, in a light embrace while I patted her back. She stopped screaming. I cradled her in my arm, rocking and swaying her. Meanwhile, her mother breastfed her other infant and somehow managed to entertain the other two in a game that was a mix of peek-a-boo and hide-and-seek. Eventually the mother—with a look on her face that indicated she now was less overwhelmed, for the moment—took her baby girl back from me. "Thank you," she said. I don't know how or why she trusted me, but she did. I don't know how or why the baby in my cradled arms calmed down, but she did.

Eight years old, I became a kid on a mission. I began reading everything I could get my hands on at the local library about poverty the world over. I learned about how a preponderance of the world's poorest die from preventable illness, malnutrition, and outright starvation, and about the untold millions, caught in the middle of violent conflicts not of their making, with no hope of living in peace or with dignity. I gave great thought to how I might best do my part to arrest or at least ameliorate this correctable tragedy. I soon set up a kiosk on the street curb in front of my house to raise money year-round for UNICEF, which serves children in the most impoverished pockets in the U.S. and abroad. It wasn't enough for me just to go door to door on Halloween as some annual feel-good activity. At my elementary school, I received special permission to set up a table in the lunch cafeteria once a week. I was determined to do what I could for the world's disadvantaged kids—from those whom UNICEF served who were not far from my own backyard, to those on the other side of the world. My goal was, and is, 1947-founded UNICEF's goal—"to build a world fit for children."

SORRY BUSINESS

I've just boarded the Boeing 777 that will take me nearly eight thousand kilometers (about five thousand miles), due south by southwest, from Tokyo to Perth, Australia. I earned my PhD from Edith Cowan University in Perth in 2010. My doctoral dissertation explored in depth how the version of the Socratic method that I've developed and spread around the world since 1996 has proved an effective means for sculpting more engaged citizens and achieving more participatory and open societies. Over the course of the five intensive years I spent researching and writing it—while juggling the writing of a popular book, *Constitution Café*, and basking in the birth of our first daughter, Cali, who would watch her dad write from her perch in a crib placed beside me—I learned so much more about the historical nuts and bolts and ethos of various iterations of the Socratic method, and about the "Socratic types" who influenced me, from Plato to Socrates (the consummate influence, needless to say), philosopher and political theorist Hannah Arendt to the social philosopher Walter Kaufmann of Princeton University, to lesser-known but no less important figures including the outstanding humanist Justus Buchler of Columbia University.

I'm returning to Western Australia for the first time since earning my PhD to hold dialogues and give presentations. I have an aisle seat on the plane. The woman beside me, Linda, is a retired nurse. She says with evident pride that she was managing nurse of an emergency room at a hospital near Perth for more than thirty-three years. She tells me she's flying back prospectively to help out at the hospital at which she worked. She wants to be on hand to pitch in when and if its staff becomes overwhelmed with patients who test positive for coronavirus (which at the time has not yet been declared a pandemic by the World Health Organization). Linda says that she has a small home on the western coast of Australia that is about a forty-five-minute drive from the hospital. She tells me she looks forward to returning there and enjoying the deep blue sunsets on the veranda of the home she'd bought three decades ago. Though she'll miss her husband (already misses him) tremendously, she says they have a plan to be in each other's physical presence every two weeks or so.

There is something about being on an airplane, even one that hasn't yet taken off, that can prompt people like Linda and me to strike up a conversation with complete strangers and share more than we otherwise might, especially if they come across as kind and themselves are in the mood for (even in need of) a good chat. Linda's husband has a government post in Tokyo for the next five years. She tells me that she remarried three years ago and is as ecstatically happy as she is deeply in love. "I never expected to have another serious relationship," she says. "It took me quite some time to become convinced, to convince myself, that this time I really had met my Prince Charming."

She tells me that eighteen years ago she'd left her position as charge nurse for her hospital's emergency room when her first husband was diagnosed with cancer. "He's an accomplished academic scholar—if you can believe it, in philosophy," she says. "For over three years, while on unpaid leave, I attended to his every need night and day. Gladly. Bill went into remission. He was able to return to a full and productive professional life. And private life, hidden private life. Two years after his return to a normal life, he left me for another woman.

"Our oldest daughter was so traumatized that she had to be hospitalized in an institution for a time. I didn't see it coming. I went through, 'How can he do this to me after all I did for him?' Then I blamed myself. Then I just was numb. My consolation was in my work and my children.

"As far as I can tell, my ex's life has gone on swimmingly. He and his wife have two children. I've hoped for karma, but I don't see it happening. Unless it's reverse karma? By that I mean, I can't imagine not having Alan as my spouse. He is that perfect for me and I hope me for him. I know I can trust him, that he'll never intentionally hurt me. More than that, he helps me discover more about myself, who I am, and what I still want to do with my life, and then does all he can to help me find a way to do it."

I tell Linda that after I finish my obligations in Western Australia, I plan to go to Uluru, also known as Ayers Rock, in the heart of the Northern Territory. I'd long regretted that I hadn't ventured there during my time in Perth for my doctoral studies. I tell her I'm determined to go there now that I'm back on this side of the world and never sure when, or if, I might come this way again.

"Uluru is where Alan and I took our honeymoon!" she says, delighted. "I had gone there once before, about a year after my divorce. I found it a place of healing. I wanted to go back again and share it with Alan."

Uluru features a natural landmark of elevated, oval-shaped sandstone that, depending on time of day, is a dazzling red or orange or brown, and rises like a monolith about 350 feet above sea level. It's considered sacred by Australia's Aboriginal people, who believe it was formed during "the Dreaming," the time period when ancestral spirits created the land and peopled it. While the Dreaming created all the earth's land masses, seas, and rivers, certain soulful places like Uluru were considered particularly sacred since the dawn of creation. Aboriginals consider Uluru a living, breathing landscape and the resting place of ancient spirits. Today, it is an Indigenous Protected Area, safeguarded by the Australian Aboriginal groups known collectively as the Anangu (which means "people"), descendants of the creators of that land and thought to be one of the (if not the) oldest surviving cultures. The Anangu to this day, in spite of earlier generations of brutal government oppression and racist-prompted dislocation, continue to live by ancient customs and laws that govern all their relationships between peoples, animals, and the land itself.

Linda tells me now that her guide, when she visited Uluru that first time, was an elder Aboriginal woman, Watyale, who was one of more than one hundred thousand children ripped away from their families and ancestral land. "The government's child removal policy didn't end until 1967, when Watyale was finally reunited with her surviving family members," she says. "She was part of the 'stolen generation'—separated from and robbed not just of her family, but her language, land, culture. She told me how she still mourns the deep hole in her life caused by the institutionalized racism."

Linda pauses before saying, "What I've experienced pales in comparison, but I did tell Watyale about my own grieving, my loss of confidence, esteem, identity. She invited me to one of their healing rites. She was letting me be part of an intimate and private and special rite in her community. I can't share much about it, but their healing process centers around the philosophy that you can't live in the past; rather, you have to let the past live in you in a way that makes life, your life, a gift again, here and now. So you have to find or make your own new path, so that the past can live within you in a way that inspires you to choose a battle and fight against today's injustices and hurts.

"Starting with the era of child removal, the Aboriginals began to refer to their shared grief as 'the Sorry Business,'" Linda says next.

"They use that term now for any kind of deep grief—and about channeling that grief in a way that can help others, especially their own youth.

"It was the honor and privilege of my life to be included by Watyale and her community in their Sorry Business rite. She said her own inspiration in dealing with her grief was the example set by Shirley Colleen Smith, who was well over ten years her senior."

A humanitarian revered by progressive Australians, Shirley Colleen Smith was an Aboriginal woman social worker and humanitarian activist who endured and then channeled the virulent racism of her day against Aboriginals to become a leading justice and welfare advocate for Aboriginal Australians. She established throughout the country legal, medical, and children's advocacy services for Aboriginals.

"My inspiration to be a nurse was my mum," she says after a short while. "Mum was a true healer. She had great passion and love for her work and tremendous caring concern and empathy for her patients. You could see it in her eyes, even after the most exhausting days. On occasion there was no childcare available, so she'd bring me to work with her. Her colleagues welcomed me with open arms, even if the rules had to be bent to have me on the premises. I was able to watch Mum in action. I knew when I was a child that I wanted to be a nurse, too, and help improve people's health and lives like she did."

Linda is starting to tell me about her newfound calling—she's a certified Qigong teacher—as our plane taxis to the runway, when I receive a call. I mistakenly hadn't yet turned off my phone. It is my principal sponsor in Australia. She tells me, despite her assurances days earlier that my events would be held as scheduled, that they have been postponed indefinitely because of the coronavirus outbreak.

I press the buzzer overhead at once to call for the flight attendant. I tell her what I just learned, and ask if I can somehow get off the plane, and even retrieve my checked-in luggage. I expect a firm (maybe even a derisive) no, as I expect it would be if I'd made such a request on one of the large U.S.-based carriers.

"Yes, of course," she says without hesitation. She springs into action. She immediately gets on the cabin phone and speaks to the captain. Then she relays to me that they will turn the plane around, park it again, let me deplane, and they will retrieve my luggage from the cargo hold. They do just that. They further offer to help change my return flight to wherever I need to go with no extra fees of any sort from their end.

There are two final places I feel I must go before returning home to my family. I never dreamed I'd be in a race against time and pandemic, but I am.

SLEEPLESS IN BUSAN

I have a fourteen-hour wait before my flight to the U.S. is set to board. I decide to stay put at the airport. I go to a twenty-four-hour lounge and fire up my laptop. I plan to write for most of the rest of the evening.

Just after 2:00 a.m., I receive this on Facebook Messenger: "Dr. Phillips, do you have any ideas about depression?"

It is from Jiyoung. Two years earlier, the vivacious, insatiably inquisitive soul, eighteen at the time, had come across and plucked off the library book shelf at the private school she attended in the Pacific Northwest my *Six Questions of Socrates*. She read it in two sittings, upon which she took it upon herself to organize what became a thriving ongoing Socrates Café when she returned to her home in Busan, South Korea—the second-largest city, situated in the southeastern corner of the mainland, known for its striking historic buildings and sparkling beaches.

By the time Jiyoung returned to school in the U.S. in early September of that year, the Socrates Café she'd started had become a mainstay, and several other participants volunteered to take turns facilitating the gatherings until her return at Christmas.

I first met Jiyoung indirectly, soon after she read my book, by way of an enthusiastic email message she'd sent to her school's humanities dean and that she cc'd me on:

> I wanted to introduce you to this amazing philosopher/writer/ adventurer/academic. . . . He has done incredible work in bringing philosophy to not only more people but also many schools. . . . Alongside writing books including *Constitution Cafe*, *Six Questions of Socrates*, and getting translated internationally, he has been an ethics fellow at Harvard, where he did some really interesting work that I can barely grasp, quite frankly.
>
> He has been instrumental in my education specifically because he provided me a model of the kind of education that I desire: more in-depth conversation, more evening of the intellectual and moral playing field between teacher and student, seriously engaging with primary texts, thinking philosophically about everything!

By the time I at last visited Jiyoung's school to speak on my efforts to "resuscitate and reinvent democracy," she had graduated. She'd hoped to make a return visit to her alma mater while I was there, but the workload at the Ivy League university at which she was now a freshman proved too demanding to permit it. What I did do, though, was lead off my presentation with an opening slide of Jiyoung. Most on hand recognized her at once and stood up and gave a loud whoop in her honor—all of which I filmed and sent to her.

Jiyoung and I periodically have had one-on-one philosophical exchanges via Skype or Facebook video. At our most recent virtual tête-à-tête some months back, we explored, "How do you know when you're in love?" She said she was finding it a challenge to discover or determine whether she was really and truly "in love."

"Is it mostly a feeling? Or also a decision?" she wanted to know. Our exploration brought to mind the dialogue I held in 1996 with my wife-to-be Ceci, when we first met at a Socrates Café and she was the only one to attend (I recount this in *Socrates Café: A Fresh Taste of Philosophy*). By the end of our discourse, Jiyoung concluded that she was head over heels in love.

Now, staring at Jiyoung's message, I am alarmed. I think immediately of my former middle school student Mindy from all those years ago in Maine. I call Jiyoung by Facebook video when I see that she's online. She answers. Her dull expression and sunken cheeks are worrisome and heartbreaking.

She sees the bustle around me and asks where I am.

"Haneda International Airport in Tokyo."

"You are kidding me. I am in South Korea. Just a two-hour flight away."

"I thought you were at your college in the U.S."

"I got permission to take the semester off," she says. "I wanted to be with my family." Jiyoung eventually tells me that she had decided, not long after our last Skype philosophical dialogue, that she was deeply in love. And then she shares that her boyfriend broke up with her several days ago. She says she's been talking regularly with a psychologist, but that even so, she is having trouble coming to terms with it.

I share with Jiyoung some of my own travails when I was about her age and went through an awful breakup. I do not tell her that, for a time, it left me in a dark place, one in which I felt I was trapped in mental and emotional quicksand. That would do her no good right now, and might cause further harm. What I do stress to her is that the person who broke up with me ultimately did me a favor, not just because I went on to meet the true love of my life, Ceci, but because, as I worked my way through the feelings of hurt and abandonment, I discovered reservoirs of inner strength that I didn't know I had.

"I hope I discover the same," she tells me. "Right now, I'm in mourning. I feel deep grief. There's a word in Korean—*han*. It means sorrow and grief and loss, but with a touch of hope."

I eventually go on to tell her that, over the longer haul, what helped me more than anything was finding a project to take on that meant so much to me that, in even the hardest of times since then, it gave me not just solace, but the wherewithal to press on. I tell Jiyoung that this renewed sense of direction and purpose came to me after reading *Letters to a Young Poet*, a collection of ten letters that the Bohemian Austrian philosophical poet Rainer Maria Rilke sent to the young officer cadet Franz Xaver Kappus. In 1929, three years after Rilke died at age fifty-one of leukemia, Kappus published them. I pull up one of the letters online that I had found particularly poignant and that seemed almost to speak directly to me. I share it with Jiyoung:

> Have patience with everything that remains unsolved in your heart. Try to love the questions themselves, like locked rooms and like books written in a foreign language. Do not now look for the answers. They cannot now be given to you because you could not live them. It is a question of experiencing everything. At present you need to live the question. Perhaps you will gradually, without even noticing it, find yourself experiencing the answer, some distant day.

"A peace or calm came over me after I came across that," I tell Jiyoung.

"At the very first Socrates Café I ever held—on the question 'What are beginnings?'—I knew then and there that this was my way of living the question, loving the questions themselves, opening locked rooms and shining light on them, and that each time I have such a gathering, I am 'experiencing the answer.'"

She asks me to read the Rilke passage to her again.

Afterward, I tell her that I recently read a set of letters of Rilke's recently published in the book *The Dark Interval: Letters on Loss, Grief and Transformation* that provided me some solace in my ongoing grief over my father's loss. I read to her a passage from a letter Rilke wrote to an intimate:

Each time we tackle something with joy, each time we open our eyes toward a yet untouched distance we transform not only this and the next moment, but we also rearrange and gradually assimilate the past inside of us. We dissolve the foreign body of pain of which we neither know its actual consistency and make-up nor how many (perhaps) life-affirming stimuli it imparts, once dissolved, to our blood!

I say to Jiyoung, "Rilke's not telling us to 'get past' our hurts, but that we give new meaning today to the irretrievable past with loving, creative acts today."

There is a light in her eyes again. "Can we just sit here in one another's presence?" she says.

"Of course."

At some point I fall asleep. When I wake up hours later, Jiyoung is no longer online. A message from her awaits: "Thank you, Dr. Phillips!!! I ended up going for a long walk in the wee hours. I have thought so much in these last hours about what we shared. What you said about not living in an irretrievable past is what I needed to hear. (That's beautiful material for a book that needs to be written to lost teens like me, by the way)."

She further writes, "Today is a new day. I'm going to hold a Socrates Café, and explore a twist on the question you asked at your very first gathering. Rather than ask, 'What are beginnings?', I will ask, 'What are new beginnings?'"

PAYBACK TIME

I am in New York City. My wife Ceci and I lived on and off in Manhattan for years, both before and just after we started a family. It's where my oldest daughter was born by midwife in 2006, exactly ten years to the day Ceci and I first met, at Roosevelt Hospital's natural childbirth center. We arrived at the hospital in the nick of time, after I managed to lock myself in my office at our apartment.

New York is where I have held scores of Socrates Cafés, most of them in Washington Square Park (once the brilliant but tormented actor Philip Seymour Hoffmann, who died in 2013 of a drug overdose, happened upon us while pushing his baby in a stroller, and took part himself). One of our Socrates Café gatherings there was held with tiki torches, beer, and lukewarm hotdogs during the widespread blackout of 2003. I also held Constitution Cafés (at the time my latest dialogue initiative, essentially offbeat mini Constitutional Conventions) at the Occupy movement's Zuccotti Park encampment. National Public Radio's Margot Adler, who died of endometrial cancer just three years later, did a feature about this (and the book by the same name), a follow-on from her piece on Socrates Café that aired in 2005. She became friends with me and my wife, and performed an unforgettably moving pagan chant at the baby shower for our daughter-to-be Cali.

Since our move to Mexico from New York in 2006 shortly after our first daughter's birth, I have been to New York sporadically but as often as time and schedule permit. I'd planned to visit the 9/11 Memorial right after its opening, while I was there to present *Constitution Café: Jefferson's Brew for a True Revolution*, at the vaunted Strand Book Store. My father's death—on September 17 of that year, on our nation's Constitution Day—forced me to cancel those plans (and much of the remainder of my book tour).

I did return to New York and its environs some months after my father's funeral to visit the 9/11 Memorial. I had told my father that I was going to do so, and it clearly meant a lot to him that I would say a prayer of remembrance at the bronze inscription of my cousin, John A. Katsimatides, a Nisyrian like me by roots who was raised mostly in Astoria. John was working that day of September 11, 2001, in his office at Cantor Fitzgerald, an investment advisor, on the 104th floor of the North Tower. He was among the nearly three thousand killed at the World Trade Center, at the Pentagon, and near Shanksville, Pennsylvania. He was thirty-one.

I did not personally know John, who by all accounts was good natured, giving, and driven to succeed. I did know his sister Anthoula, starting from the time I presented to the Nisyrian Society of New York and she interviewed me for a Greek radio program about my Socrates Café effort. My multitalented cousin is an accomplished actress for stage, television, and screen, as well as a producer (her newest documentary is on the Academy Award–winning Greek actress Olympia Dukakis). When John was killed, she already was grieving the loss of her younger brother Mike, an ebullient yet sensitive soul who felt all the hurts of the world and had committed suicide two years earlier. After the terrorist attack, Anthoula became director of family relations at the Lower Manhattan Development Corporation. She pitched in with every ounce of energy and passion to the rebuilding and the healing effort. Besides accepting an appointment to the board of the National September 11 Memorial and Museum, Anthoula formed a nonprofit in memory of her brothers—the JAM for Life Foundation (JAM is short for Johnny and Mikey)—that "seeks to promote . . . music education, cancer research, aid for underprivileged youth, suicide prevention and the rights of crime victims by donating funds . . . to charities that embody the spirt, character and lives of John and Mike . . . and promote the well-being of the community while perpetuating John and Mike's legacy and honoring the lives of two special individuals." (This was the main inspiration that prompted me to start my own project to honor my father's legacy, the annual Alexander Phillips Arete Award.)

It is March 20, my late father's birthday.

On this visit, as all previous ones, I seek out the name of cousin John on the bronze parapet. After hours of reflection and remembrance, I take the DeCamp bus to Montclair, New Jersey, home not only of Stephen Colbert of *Late Show* fame but also where I inaugurated my first Socrates Café, in 1996, at a cozy coffeehouse on Bloomfield Avenue, and that still meets weekly a quarter century later. I was invited to preside over the philosophical festivities. It's the first time I have been back there in years. Many who were part of our "charter" group about twenty-five years ago have moved elsewhere (many of them establishing Socrates Cafés in their new locales) or have passed away, including Bill Hayes, a retired postal worker who became a close friend. Bill had never read a word of philosophy before he began attending, and wound up returning to college with the aim of earning a degree in the discipline (he developed a particular affinity for the American pragmatist-naturalist philosophical tradition). On the night I am facilitating the Socrates Café in Montclair, it feels like a homecoming, not only because this is where it all began, but most of all because there are still several on hand from all those years ago. It's also wonderful to become acquainted with kindred spirits who've just recently discovered the joys of philosophical inquiry the Socratic way and have found Socrates Café a worthy antidote for providing their insatiable questioning natures with a weekly fix. My "grandiose" plan in 1996 was to just start this one Socrates Café in Montclair. It is humbling and thrilling that we now have hundreds of ongoing gatherings around the world, with more forming all the time, after all these years.

It was late that night at the twenty-four-hour diner where we'd gathered before everyone drifted off. Everyone except for me and Frank. At the formal gathering, he was as intensely immersed in every word uttered, and as intensely silent, as my own father characteristically was whenever he'd attended. Frank and I had begun a unique friendship after I'd initiated a Socrates Café at the maximum security prison at which he had been serving a fifteen-year sentence for armed robbery.

A psychiatric social worker who has been a longtime participant in the Montclair Socrates Café paved the way for it. She was convinced it was what inmates needed and witnessed firsthand at what became ongoing gatherings—she and other staff took the reins of it after my inaugural inquiry there—how it was changing for the better inmates' outlooks, attitudes, openness to thinking thoroughly about and through things from many perspectives, and how this in turn led to marked changes for the better in their character and spirit.

About a month after my visit, I received a letter. The return address had an inmate number, but no name. It was from Frank. He shared that the Socrates Café was making a difference. "It's helped me see more clearly," he wrote. "It gives me ideas about other people's thoughts. I look at things one way, and I discover that the guy sitting right beside me, who I thought I knew well, has a very different way of thinking about the question. After considering where he's coming from, and why he's coming from where he's coming from, it sometimes changes my entire outlook. I see the question, and the world, in a different light." Frank shared with me that he'd loaned the copy of *Socrates Café* that I'd signed and given to him to another inmate who had been put in solitary after a fight. "He read it word for word. Said it changed his whole way of seeing things, too."

In correspondences that followed, one of them after that year's commemoration of the 9/11 tragedy, Frank wrote: "I remember seeing from a prison window the smoke billowing from the direction of the World Trade Centers on September 11, 2001. When I learned what happened, I felt anger and helplessness. I read about all the heroics, and here I was in prison. Because of my stupidity those years back, I couldn't pitch in and be of service."

Frank completed the mandatory ten years of his fifteen-year sentence, and then the rest was reduced because of his exemplary behavior. He left prison with a GED and associate degrees in English and in business management. His goal was to become a first responder. He was informed he'd have to wait several more years, because of his felony conviction. "I totally get it," he wrote. "I'm used to waiting. I won't give up on that goal. Even when I achieve it, I'll never be able to pay back to society the debt I owe. There is another way I'll be of service in the meantime."

Frank joined the military. After he went through a comprehensive series of interviews, exams, and psychological tests, he was granted a waiver and permitted to enlist for an initial four-year commitment. Frank had expected he'd be deployed to Iraq or Afghanistan. But after his superiors reviewed a written essay that was part of one of his exams, they decided they could put his exceptional writing skills to optimal use by assigning him to a communications department to compose reports and letters and such for top-level brass. Frank remained stateside the entire four years of his enlistment. "It was just good to be able to serve, to begin paying off my debt in the way they thought best," he wrote.

By the time of this latest visit of mine to New York and New Jersey, Frank is a seasoned first responder. He had been living with his second-oldest daughter. "She's all about forgiveness," he'd once written. "Welcomed me with open arms when I was released from prison." He said his other children were upset at first with their sibling that she'd taken him in but, over time, became reconciled to it. He tells me he is no longer living with his daughter, who had married and is pregnant, but that he has a nice apartment nearby. He is beyond excited about becoming a grandfather. Frank never entered into another serious romantic relationship. He said he wanted to devote all his spare time and energy to his children, if they ever needed him (they did, over time, all of them), and his grandchildren.

"The prison I was in was originally called a reformatory, and in my case, that it was," he says. "I left a reformed man. I didn't run away from my past. I've taken that past, owned it, owned up to it. I wouldn't be who I am without it. Cliché but true. Like I've said, I'll never completely pay my debt to society. I'll always have regrets, lasting regrets, but I wouldn't be who I am now if I hadn't been who I was then."

I tell Frank about my visit to the 9/11 Memorial, that it is my late father's birthday, and for the first time, about my father's death and my journeys to learn more about souls of goodness, and how to rediscover joy and love and bearing and such within my still-deep anguish.

Frank stays silent for a long while. "I fear for the world of our children and grandchildren. So much hate and anger and rage. So many, including from your and my generations, can't see past the nose on their faces. Self-entitlement is all. They'll do anything— anything—if a dollar is to be had. You know I know what I'm talking about."

He looks in the direction of where the World Trade Center once stood. "To this day many view those terrorists as heroes and martyrs. Celebrations are held in their honor. They've caused a world of hurt that for many thousands will never go away. But I've caused a world of hurt too. I'll spend the rest of my life trying to make up for that with good works.

"It's all about making a decision, every day, to 'break good.' The Socrates Café tonight was about, 'What are the best opportunities?' For me, they're ones that give me a new chance to take a step in the direction of 'getting it right'— by that I mean that the best ending to each day is when I reflect on my day's deeds and actions, and I can honestly conclude I've taken a step in that direction."

He has a sip of coffee and then says, "Chris, I don't know if you can ever forgive, at least completely, but you can't be consumed by the extreme haters and betrayers, especially those you were once close to. I see the hurt and anguish; it's written all over your face. You don't deserve it. Your loved ones don't deserve it. From what you've shared about your father, I can say with confidence that he'd agree with me. Don't let people like this 'win.' This person is still filled with self-loathing. No amount of money can fill that empty hole inside. I feel grateful I was capable of learning my lesson, of taking responsibility. But some won't, and some can't. I met many of them in prison."

I think back to what Cornel West told me during our recent visit. I have it transcribed, and I share it with Frank:

> Never stop loving that person you're telling me about, my brother. There are those who spiritually do not receive the kind of love that they ought in their own families and communities and the larger societies. Never forget Dostoevsky's definition of love in *Brothers Karamazov*: hell is suffering from the incapacity to love. Such people think of themselves as so worthless, as not worthy of love.

This brings a thoughtful smile to Frank's face. "Couldn't have said it better. And it's what your father would say to you now, if he could."

UNFORGIVENESS

I've thought a great deal about forgiveness and paying your debt to society since my encounter at my philosopher's stone with the indigo child in Maine—learning about his mother's incredible capacity to forgive, and how over time it also led him and his father to do the same—and now with Frank.

I have also asked myself: What would Socrates do?

Socrates managed the feat of facing an ignominious death—and doing so free of resentment. But he wasn't full of forgiveness. For Socrates, forgiveness of those who'd committed the cardinal sin against him—orchestrating the death of an innocent man—was beside the point. As he puts it in the *Apology* to the jury of his peers that convicted him of a capital crime deemed to merit his execution:

> You can be sure that if you kill the sort of man I am, you will not harm me more than yourselves. Neither Meletus nor Anytus

[his principal accusers of corrupting the youth and of impiety] can harm me in any way . . . for I do not think that it is permitted that a better man be harmed by a worse. . . . . I think he is doing himself much greater harm doing what he is doing now, attempting to have a man executed unjustly.

IIis is a radical theory of unforgiveness. No need to forgive—much less to punish retributively—if you subscribe to Socrates's view that no true harm has been done to you, that your transgressors are in fact doing more harm to themselves, even if they willfully put a premature end to your life in the process. To Socrates, what was paramount in life was healthiness of soul. In part, you manifest such healthiness by never stooping to the level of those who would do you harm, and even *do* do you harm.

The other marvel to me, besides his revolutionary philosophy of unforgiveness, is that Socrates didn't heap judgment or scorn on his transgressors. Socrates never labeled or lashed out verbally at Anytus or Meletus, didn't characterize them as wicked or evil. As someone who knew himself thoroughly, he long ago had grasped the truth that there is little if any wall between those considered wicked and those good. A circumstance here, another there, and he might well have been like them. His soul was so healthy and brimming with goodness.

The renowned parable of the pitiless servant in the New Testament's Gospel of Matthew begins with Peter asking, "'Lord, how many times shall I forgive my brother when he sins against me? Up to seven times?" Jesus answered, "I tell you, not seven times, but seventy times seven."

Hannah Arendt asserts in *The Human Condition* that "the discoverer of the role of forgiveness in the realm of human affairs was Jesus of Nazareth," to her the paragon of the power of forgiveness. "The fact that he made this discovery in a religious context and articulated it in religious language is no reason to take it any less seriously in a strictly secular sense."

Socrates without question would have agreed with this assertion of Arendt's, and would also have embraced wholeheartedly the New Testament's John 8:7 (KJV): "He that is without sin among you, let him first cast a stone."

By that ethos, then, if you have been betrayed, you should ask yourself: Have I betrayed too? If you reply, "Yes, but it's different in my case." Then ask: Different how? Was it nonetheless a betrayal? Was someone hurt by it? What if you have been lied to in a damaging way? You might ask yourself: Have I lied? If you reply, "Well, yes, but it didn't do nearly as much harm." But did it do harm to someone? Could it have? Did it benefit you in a way that it shouldn't have?

I may not be able to die proudly, no more than my dad. All the more reason to act in ways while I am alive, however much or little time I have, that I know would make Dad proud. What would that be? To do what many can't, including him. He would expect me to forgive the unforgivable.

LIFE AND DEATH CAFÉ

I'm seated in a tight circle with a baker's dozen, if my quick count is accurate. Tight but not airtight. I'd like to say that those here with me came at my invitation, but perhaps they've done so more at their own bidding than mine. At least two or three more can still squeeze in, if those on hand are inclined to make room. Some present are impossible not to recognize. Others go out of their way to be incognito.

The room in which we find ourselves is not dissimilar to Gabriel Garcia Marquez's constructed world in *One Hundred Years of Solitude*, with attached rooms connected by doors in which one opens "into another that was just the same, the door of which would open into another that was just the same, and into another exactly alike, and so on to infinity." All the rooms are identical except "the room of reality," the room to which you have to somehow find your way back to lest you "stay there forever," trapped in a "gallery of parallel mirrors," a fate that is a kind of death, or worse than death, because you lose all touch with reality, with yourself, with others.

Traditional notions of time and space aren't altogether effaced at our gathering, but they have assumed secondary status at best. What I can say with certainty is that no one here is a mere figment of my or anyone else's imagination. Just as I can say beyond a shadow of a doubt that all of us are haunted.

"How should you die?" is the question hovering in our midst. No one in particular proposed it. No, all of us did. It is our reason for being here now.

The first to speak is Argentina Apollo. His real name is Vincent Denigris, but he named himself professionally after the Olympian god of archery, music, poetry, art, oracles, and . . . plague. My dad and I had gone many times during my childhood and youth to see in action this incomparably acrobatic star of the World Wide Wrestling Federation. Apollo always took time to sign autographs in our program and speak with us after his matches (almost always big wins).

My dad, a WWF fanatic, is clearly thrilled that Argentina Apollo, who tells him to just call him Apollo, is on hand. Dad pulls his chair beside the former wrestling great and engages in a one-way animated chat. He's instructing Apollo that one of Socrates's favorite places to hold dialogues was at the *palaestra*, a gymnasium used primarily for that oldest sport, wrestling. Dad informs Apollo that Socrates was enthralled that wrestling demanded both brawns and brain, requiring both collaboration and fierce competition between its opponents. Dad further tells him that in Plato's *Euthyphro*, Socrates's friends rib him about hanging out at the wrestling gym, where Plato himself is said to have become smitten with the sport, to the extent that he excelled in it. Apollo listens politely and from time to time says, "You don't say" at just the right moments, though his demeanor suggests he isn't hearing anything he doesn't know already. I clear my throat to bring them back to our dialogue. I remind them what the question is.

"I died of a heart attack at age forty-six," our erstwhile idol says after a pause. "Yes, by that time, I had achieved many of my professional dreams. But forty-six? No, I definitely shouldn't have died then, as I did, when I did. Nothing that I was aware of indicated I was a heart attack candidate. I felt great. Great! I still feel anger and resentment over dying too young. I was in the throes of learning to play trumpet, and was forming a mariachi group, the Apollos. Then: game of life over."

"Our father died after just turning fifty-eight," says Dad's reticent, enigmatic sister Maria, whom I have always called Aunt Mary. She herself died at age sixty-six of a stroke. My dad discovered his younger sister's body, as he did his older brother, who had died of a stroke the previous year.

"One minute, Alec"—she calls my dad "Alec"—"and I were playing tag with our father Philip," Maria says, "and the next, he collapsed like a rag doll. *Should* he have died that day, in that way? He'd never had a thorough physical exam in his life. No time or money for such extravagances."

"Fifty-eight years old," Dad says. He shakes his head. "Just when he was on the verge of living his dream as a stage performer."

He then says, "I always said that if I lived more than fifty-eight years, all the time allotted to me after that would be a gift."

Alexander Phillips was "gifted" twenty additional years. He looks at me. "Should I have had more years? Should I have died when I did, as I did? That's an open question. But the deed is done."

"Is it?" I say. "Then why doesn't peace descend on me?"

Dad sees the anguish on my face. Sees that I won't forgive myself for not being there for him. He wants to reach out and embrace me, make everything okay.

Only then do I notice that someone else looms here with us, just outside the circle, almost eavesdropping—hollow, nameless, more a palpable absence than a presence. No one makes a move to open up the circle in case he wants to sit among us and join in.

"Dad," I say. He's holding an internal conversation. His lips move in an animated way as he says something to this someone, not too pleasant by all indications, just under his breath as he jabs the air with a forefinger.

"Dad."

He returns to what one might normally assume is the land of the living. "I shouldn't have died as I did," he says at last, looking at each of us, "but I did."

Dad considers and reconsiders. "Perhaps I did die as I should have. Some things that I said, that I did, as a father, a husband, a man . . ."

William Faulkner weighs in by reading from one of his own works. "'I can remember how when I was young I believed death to be a phenomenon of the body; now I know it to be merely a function of the mind.' Dr. Peabody. *As I Lay Dying*. 'The nihilists say it is the end; the fundamentalists, the beginning; when in reality it is no more than a single tenant or family moving out of a tenement or a town.'"

"How does that relate to our question, 'How should I die?'" I ask, deferential, in awe that someone of his stature is among us.

"If it's a function of the mind, then it can be the end and the beginning," Dad says before Faulkner can get a word in edgewise. Faulkner nods his head. It dawns on me that this is the first time Dad has ever said a word at one of the many dialogues that I've presided over and that he has attended over the years. "Or neither. Or either. If you're a nihilist, it's the end, if a fundamentalist, the beginning. If a single tenant or family, then it's like my childhood family, moving out of one tenement, making space there, but moving in presumably to another, taking up space there."

"If that's so, then 'should' has nothing to do with it?" I ask.

I hope Dad will answer my question in the affirmative.

Instead he directs his gaze to Socrates, who sits in spellbound silence. It seems a little cheeky to me, but Dad takes it upon himself to quote the philosopher's own insights as passed down to us in Plato's *Apology*: "'What would not a man give to converse with

Orpheus and Musaeus and Hesiod and Homer? Nay, if this be true, let me die again and again!'"

Socrates, eyebrows arched, says now, "Well, maybe Orpheus and Musaeus and Hesiod and Homer aren't here, but this is pretty good company." His eyes rest in particular on Argentina Apollo, who is oblivious that he is the apple of the sage's eye.

A long silence ensues. "There is no should on matters of dying," Dad says. "There should be, but there isn't. Not in the world to-day." He leaves it at that.

Time passes. Aunt Mary eventually says to him, "Alec, remember the time we hopped on a train when we were kids? We thought it was like an amusement car ride. It was so fun, sitting in the caboose, our legs swinging over the edge while the train clattered over the tracks. But then it started heading out of town! We'd lost track of time. We were absorbed in pretending we were on a great adventure and inventing stories about where we were going. In a world of our own.

"We hopped off just in time, had to walk several miles to get back home. The train was heading to New Orleans.

"That was living," Aunt Mary says next. "Alec and I did something we weren't supposed to do, but that didn't do any harm to anyone else. Something we got away with, thankfully, and that didn't cause harm to us or anyone else. Something out of the ordinary. I later wrote a story about it for a class assignment. My teacher thought I was making it up. Gave me an A+ for excellent use of my imagination.

"But it also answers 'how we should die,'" she says to me. "That one childhood experience of mine made me feel like, 'If I die tomorrow, it'll be okay, because I did something daring and exciting and out of the ordinary.' I know it wasn't world changing, but it changed my world. So, perhaps it answers the question, 'How should we *not* die?' My answer is, not before we go on at least one grand adventure. That single childhood experience made me a little more daring and bold as I went on with life. Even on my most dull and boring days, all I had to do was conjure up that memory, and it gave me a needed boost."

I expect Dad to laugh along with her at the shared experience—one he'd never told me about—maybe follow up with a comment on his own. He is so lost in thought, I'm not sure he had even heard her.

Socrates was relatively old, as was my dad, no matter how they died. Given that, should they feel less anger for the way their lives ended?

Socrates for one, the epitome of nonresentment, nonetheless couldn't help but point out, as Plato records, that "in another world they do not put a man to death for asking questions: assuredly not." Which is to say: you should not ever be put to death merely for asking questions.

Yet he was sentenced to death for that very reason. In the *Apology*, he says his goodbyes without regret: "The hour of departure has arrived, and we go our separate ways, I to die, and you to live. Which of these two is better only God knows."

The rest of those present do not show any inclination to speak. I have long since learned not to press anyone to do so. Several are friends from my high school days, several of whom, like me, were on the wrestling team. After graduation, one went to a prestigious university, eventually dropping out—he spent more time playing guitar than he did attending classes—and becoming a housepainter. Mark died in his early fifties of an alcohol-related disease. His wife, grief stricken, died suddenly soon afterward. Another friend on hand now was a perennial medal winner at our statewide wrestling championship. Scott became a bricklayer after his high school days, and died in his late forties, of a nervous system disorder. Another was a construction worker who lived not far from my father. He died in his early fifties in a freak accident, falling from the roof of a house he and his team were in the final stages of building. Another, Robert, died from cancer shortly after high school graduation. The applause had been loud and long as he made his way to the stage, leaning against a cane to support himself, to receive his diploma. They were all inordinately thoughtful souls. They never were much for talking to begin with. They weren't antisocial but preferred to listen to what others had to say. I learned a great deal from them about the art of listening. I don't ask them how or why it is that they are here today, all of us together for the first time in forty years.

We pass around a bottle of ouzo, Greece's potent alcoholic drink that tastes like licorice, as well as a bottle of mineral water for those who prefer not to drink alcohol. The last time I was part of a gathering in which a bottle of strong spirits was passed around like this, among all those on hand, was at William Faulkner's grave in Oxford, Mississippi, which I visited with the noted Southern authors Willie Morris and Barry Hannah, and my dear friend Alex Haley, whom I had accompanied on the trip there. The Pulitzer Prize–winning author of *Roots*, who helped me get my start as a writer and who died of a massive heart attack in 1992, left his vast estate in such disarray and arrears that most of his assets were then sold on auction block.

I have no idea how much time, if any, passes. Most who attend begin to fade. Except Dad. At last, he says, "Son, I'm sorry, so sorry, that we didn't get to say our goodbyes. But you know how much I love you, how proud I am of you.

"Keep earning your rest," he says next. "Keep doing all you can to make the world one in which more and more can die with dignity."

I can't make out completely what Dad says next—something to the effect that I shouldn't mourn that I'm starting to forget him. He's rudely interrupted by a loudspeaker announcement. Our plane flight originating in New York is set to land in Tampa, Florida.

As I exit, for now, our room of irreality, to make one last visit before I return home, I receive a text message from Frank. "New York is now in complete lockdown. I just received an 'all hands on deck' call for EMTs. Payback time."

REMEMBRANCE OF FUTURE THINGS REMEMBERED

Close to the end of Gabriel Garcia Marquez's *One Hundred Years of Solitude*, the "Melquiades manuscript" is discovered. On the parchment manuscript, the history of the Buendia family is recorded, "one hundred years ahead of time." The wizened gypsy friend of the patriarch Jose Arcadio Buendia who'd composed it "had not put events in the order of man's conventional time, but had concentrated a century of daily episodes in such a way that they coexisted in one instant." Illusion, memory, prophecy, what passes for present reality, are entwined in such a seamless way that the events recounted are as or more believable—more "natural"—than if they'd been told chronologically.

Much ado is made about remembering the past to imagine the future. But Jorge Luis Borges and Gabriel Garcia Marquez would join me in querying: What about remembering the future to imagine the past? Efforts to remember in a past-dwelling, episodic way even our most beloved who are no longer with us are doomed to fail to some extent, no matter how much we might plaster our homes and hearts with vivid remembrances. But if we remember them in our future, the past comes alive, not as a fait accompli, but reimagined and remade.

What we do—our words and works and deeds—tomorrow and tomorrow and tomorrow gives new meaning to all that came before. Psychologists have a term, *chronosthesia*, to denote "mental time travel": it is every bit as much about the future as the past. The human mind, cognitive scientists and neuroscientists have discovered, can project itself to future points in time just as deftly and effortlessly as they can to past ones.

At minimum, the imagined future is on par with the imagined past. At minimum, everything is imagined, even the present, to a degree. It's not that all is relative, but that all is relational, and to some degree imagined—this can be to the good, or the evil. Hitler imagined concentration camps and made them real; others joined him in constructing it in the present. The emphasis is traditionally on forecasting the future by recasting or reexperiencing the past—but it can cut both or myriad ways, and one cannot just recast but forecast the past by experiencing the future, in a way that drives our present.

Just ask Shakespeare. The scholar Harold Bloom can "hardly see how one can begin to consider Shakespeare," a nonpareil mental time traveler,

> without finding some way to account for his pervasive presence in the most unlikely contexts: here, there, and everywhere at once. He is a system of northern lights, an aurora borealis visible where most of us will never go. Libraries and playhouses (and cinemas) cannot contain him; he has become a spirit or "spell of light," almost too vast to apprehend.

Those with schizophrenia would apprehend. Their conceptions of time range from ones in which past, present, and future either are collapsed, or outright stand still, or cease to exist altogether. As Shakespeare observes in *As You Like It*, "Time travels in divers places with divers persons."

When Shakespeare says in *As You Like It* that "all the world's a stage," surely he is talking about the mental world as much as any other dimension or construct. Shakespeare and Garcia Marquez know that what we take for tenses are on the same plane, interchangeable and oscillating, none with priority or even precedence.

SO LONG, FAREWELL

"Adieu, adieu, Hamlet," his father's ghost says. "Remember me."

Hester Lees-Jeffries, a Cambridge fellow, asserts in *Shakespeare and Memory* that our memories of our beloved who have died

> may, for a time, live on; they may even, for a brief moment, reanimate the dead, but undifferentiated bones (and eventually dust) are all that will remain. For all the disquiet expressed at various points by Hamlet, Ophelia, Laertes and the Ghost, no human ceremony can alter the fact of mortality, or safeguard against the once-beloved dead being forgotten.

This is only so if we place a premium on episodic memory. You don't have to be dead to be forgotten. What's more, you can differ on the accuracy of something that happened a minute ago (if you haven't forgotten it altogether). People who witness up close the same car accident can have widely varying accounts.

In the case of our nearest and dearest who are physically gone, there is something that doesn't supplant but can help conquer or overcome all lost memories and accounts of them and much unfinished business: love. Out of that boundless, bottomless love born of irreplaceable loss, out of that anguish, pain, hurt that may never go away—depending on circumstances of death and other "factors"—and that can increase with the passing of time, even as concrete memories fade, for as long as you live you can act in ways that deepen and expand that love. You can do so with moral imagination and moral courage and the near-certain knowledge that most of us won't know when our own time is up. You do it for them in particular, but for many others who've come and gone, for others still here, and even more so for those to come, through loving acts.

What constitutes "loving acts"? Among other things, they are those that can serve as bridges among our fellow humans, that cultivate our more humane sensibilities and sensitivities, so that when we act on and in the world, we do so with the idea that we're taking into keen account and with careful consideration others who might be impacted—and in ways that not only do no harm, but potentially do some good.

Nothing grandiose necessary. It can be something as "simple" as taking the time to learn the story of someone you've greeted countless times but have never gotten to know—perhaps a waiter, a colleague, a street vendor—or someone you may never have a chance to know again—a fellow passenger on a bus or plane. In my experience, there are few greater gifts than asking someone to share some of their story, and to listen to it with all you have, without judging or labeling. It can transform all involved in the "transaction," and even more so when you ask others to share not only some of their chronological tale, but their moral story, and how they have come to hold the values and code that they do.

FROM THE CRADLE TO THE GRAVE

The grave plot for my dad at Cycadia Cemetery in Tarpon Springs, Florida, is immediately to the left of his mother's, my *yaya*, who died in 1972 at age seventy-seven, and beside that of his younger sister Maria and her husband, my uncle John Bates. My grandfather Philip's grave is a stone's throw away.

I kneel for hours in front of Dad's simple granite headstone, which also includes a special marker in honor of his military service.

Let me tell you about Dad while I'm here.

Shortly before Alexander Phillips entered the world, his parents and older brother moved from Charleston, South Carolina, to live for a time in a poor Greek enclave in the small struggling southern city of Hopewell, Virginia. Though no longer by the sea, they at least were surrounded by the Appomattox River. Their subsistence life in Charleston and then Hopewell, while not as grinding and numbing perhaps as in Nisyros, was nonetheless not the reason they'd left kith and kin in Greece to start life anew in the U.S. It turned out, in coastal Charleston and then in Hopewell, opportunities for economic advancement were scarce. To add insult to injury, southern racists residing in and around these cities did all they could to make them feel unwelcome; the Ku Klux Klan led the charge, depicting them as interlopers and scapegoating them as job robbers, though nothing could have been further from the truth (far more often than not, they took on backbreaking work that locals refused).

Dad entered the world in Hopewell, Virginia, in 1933, and his sister Maria the following year. It was the tail end of the Great Depression. Times were about to appear brighter. In 1939, his family made its way to Tampa, Florida. Philip was drawn by the promise of good work. A job at an upscale restaurant had been offered to him by a relative, a successful restaurateur, in the city's gradually reviving business and entertainment center. Though Tampa was in the South, it was far more cosmopolitan than most cities in that region of the U.S. Best of all, it had a large Greek population, all of whom looked out for one another. But they did not make their exit from Hopewell before permanent damage had been done to my dad. He'd been teased cruelly by his public school classmates there for having a thick Greek accent. The severe lisp that resulted from this trauma was one he never completely overcame. He exhibited it at times even in his later years when under inordinate stress (as I write this, I realize I hadn't heard Dad speak with a lisp for a number of years, until we spoke by phone, just before he died, the last time we ever talked).

In Tampa, Dad's family stayed put, their days of dislocation at last behind them. They lived what by most accounts was a pleasant life in its way, even if hardscrabble by many yardsticks. Although they resided in a cramped apartment in a housing tenement, to them it was a homey place tucked within a vibrant and close-knit neighborhood. My grandfather Philip was a natural at his job, a solicitous waiter who also delighted his clients as a comic and singer. He sported a white tuxedo at the swank restaurant. Meanwhile, Yaya created a profession for herself; she was said to be the first in that region to put out her shingle as teacher (and proselytizer; to her the two went hand in glove) of Greek language and culture. Yaya was

so beloved and popular that she enjoyed the luxury of a long waiting list of prospective students. She held her classes in a large
storage room that she converted into a bright space with shelves
lined with books and posters of the greatest Greek artists, philosophers, poets. Her husband was as much relieved as he was thrilled
that she'd found a pursuit from which she derived immense pleasure, though he himself took little to no interest in Greek culture. He
was the earthy one, she the cerebral one.

My grandmother was as content as could be expected, even if
her heart lay elsewhere. My uncle Jimmy told me that his mother
had written a poem, "6,051," that he'd discovered folded up into a
small square of paper at the bottom of her jewelry box. The poem,
he said, was about the 6,051-mile-long bridge she built between her
heart, in Tampa, and the heart of someone she left behind on Nisyros.

All things considered, 1942 was shaping up to be a banner year
for the Philipou family—now, officially, the Phillips family, what
with their last name summarily changed by Ellis Island bureaucrats.
The Great Depression was receding into the past; Tampa's business
and entertainment districts in Ybor City were undergoing a renais-
sance. Bright lights showcased the strip on Franklin Street. What's
more, at long last, my grandfather and Yaya, years after their initial
application—which had been delayed repeatedly after Philip's
internment on Ellis Island—had become bona fide U.S. citizens.
Philip considered it a propitious sign that their official approval
came on February 29, 1940, leap-year day.

On January 2, 1942, my grandfather Philip celebrated his fifty-
eighth birthday. He and his wife actually had enough money, and
time, to go out on the town for a night away from their brood.
Things were looking up on all fronts. As my grandfather worked
double shifts at the restaurant, earning generous but well-deserved
tips for his impeccable service, and as Yaya plied away at her
teaching labor of love, they chipped away at the walls of poverty

that had enveloped them all their lives. Philip somehow managed to steal time to audition for various openings announced for performing artists and such at the variety shows staged at local theaters and casinos. Never say die, he had not given up after all these years on realizing his dream of becoming a stage artist of some sort.

Dad's parents were on the verge of saving enough money to move out of the projects—on 1209 West Platt Street, just over a block from a bustling highway in south-central Tampa—and buy their own home. Philip had been offered a job, a good-paying one, as part of an in-house performing troupe at the Tampa Bay Hotel Casino. Eight days after my grandfather turned fifty-eight, his dream at last had become a reality. My dad, six at the time, and his five-year-old sister Maria danced a jig in celebration with their father. They circled round and round in the living room, singing and dancing in grand fashion. When Philip collapsed to the floor without warning, my dad and his sister took it for granted he was playacting. They laughed and hopscotched over him again and again, enjoying this new twist in their spontaneous celebration.

Yaya and Uncle Jimmy entered the apartment a few minutes later. Yaya saw her husband on the floor and screamed. My grandfather was dead of a heart attack. Philip had never had a thorough medical exam in his life, only the cursory ones at Ellis Island.

Dad found himself thrust into the role of breadwinner. His mother, though mourning, easily slipped into the role of matriarch; Greece was matrilineal, and as the oldest among her siblings, she had a long-practiced authority. Yaya already had big plans for Dad's brother, older by a decade. Her command to Dad was one of all work and little play, so that Uncle Jimmy could matriculate in college and then continue to law school. Dad threw himself into this new lot in life with an indomitable drive and spirit, never wallowing in what others might well consider a woe-is-me lot. As a youngster, he hawked the *Tampa Bay Times* on busy downtown street corners and delivered groceries. He was even featured in an article in the *Times* when a customer gave him a rare quarter of considerable worth.

Dad still found a way to engage in play, though not of the sort typical for children his age from higher socioeconomic strata. It proved to be a lucrative form of play. Dad taught himself to play piano by ear. Boogie-woogie tunes were his forte. The ones he heard and tapped his feet to outside of taverns and dance halls while he sold newspapers. He became so proficient that he soon was a regular fixture as a pianist at those venues. My dad was a natural as a performer; his father would no doubt have considered him a chip off the old block. Blessed with a photographic memory, in no time Dad was tickling the ivories expertly and passionately to complex tunes, including his favorite, Meade Lux Lewis's "Roll 'Em." Dad gave his all to his various labors, with love and abandon. He did not feel the slightest pity for himself, did not feel he was missing out on a thing or had been dealt an unfair hand. He still somehow found time to excel in public school. Though he could only attend class the first part of the day, he was not penalized; Dad kept up with all his assignments, and was a straight-A student. Sleep was an infrequent luxury.

In 1950, my uncle Jimmy was called to serve still another tour of duty, this time in the Korean conflict. His law school studies were put on hiatus. Now Yaya placed her hopes for financial security in the workaday world in my dad. He diffidently told her that his aim was to own a grocery store–café with a large enough space to also have an enclave for a piano bar. Yaya would have none of it. She handed him an ad she had torn from the very newspaper that he sold. It was from the vaunted Newport News Shipyard in Newport News, Virginia, the world's largest shipyard with a city's worth of employees, located in the peninsula of the commonwealth. It announced that it was seeking students for its newly opened Apprentice School. It needed stellar students who could be trained in the cutting-edge art and science of shipbuilding for clients including the U.S. military and leading private maritime industries.

Yaya told Dad in no uncertain terms that he was going to fill out the enrollment application, that he would be accepted, and that he would be trained to design ships. That's what happened. Soon after arriving in Newport News, Dad met my mother, Margaret Ann, a soon-to-be high school graduate who would matriculate in nursing school. They married on April 10, 1955. Madly in love and more inspired than ever, on top of his exhaustive studies, Dad taught himself the ins and outs of the world of investing. He began to sell mutual funds to shipyard workers and fellow students. He also found time to serve as Apprentice School class president, to play in every sport the program offered—basketball, baseball, football— and excel in each (usually he was team captain), all the while learning a valuable trade in ship design.

From there, Dad was drafted into the army, where he developed still another skill, radio operator. Fortunately it was peacetime. Soon after his tour of duty ended, he was hired by the Department of the Navy, at its Supervisor of Shipbuilding, which oversaw the construction at the Newport News Shipyard of all the navy vessels contracted to be built there. He also became the first-ever person to graduate from Christopher Newport College by earning his degree by taking exclusively nighttime classes. A lasting image of mine: my father sitting alone in the wee hours at our dining room table, college texts spread out everywhere, his nose buried deeply in them. After returning home from a heavy day at work, and then a long evening at night school, he would have a quick meal, then pore over his textbooks, not just to excel in his college classes but also to pass the exam to become a professional engineer. Dad had developed a passion for the world of electrical engineering while at the Apprentice School. It didn't offer a specialty area in that field, so he mastered the subject himself, teaching himself complex math principles as they applied to electrical engineering and shipbuilding, what with his photographic memory, much like he'd learned complex musical scores as a child.

Dad came honestly by his passion and enthusiasm for the world of shipbuilding. Given what he'd shared with pride about his own maritime forebears, it was in his DNA. Little wonder he was disappointed when he was drafted into the army rather than the navy. Several years after Dad left the Newport News Shipyard, he found a home with the navy when he embarked on what would turn out to be a stellar career with the Department of the Navy. We had to move to the Washington, D.C., area, where we lived several years; and then, in order for him to advance still further up the bureaucratic totem pole, back to Newport News. While it was difficult to adjust to life again in the South in far less cosmopolitan environs than the greater D.C. area, it provided the most promising and expeditious pathway for Dad's dream of being both a supervisor of shipbuilding for all major navy seacraft, and of putting his electrical engineer skills to use, to become a reality.

By the time Dad retired in 1999, he did so as the longtime chief of the electrical division of the Supervisor of Shipbuilding. In that capacity, Dad—who'd been nominated for a prestigious award by the American Society of Naval Engineers for major contributions he'd single-handedly made to advances in their field—oversaw all the electrical design and installation for our military's nuclear aircraft carrier fleets. I went to each and every aircraft carrier christening with Dad, starting with that of the USS *Nimitz* in 1972. I was in awe as I stood feet away from dignitaries, including U.S. senators and top White House officials. I enjoyed buffets featuring delicacies that included shrimp almost as large as the size of my hand— and some of which Dad, the poor boy still part of him, wrapped in napkins and stuffed in the pockets of his suits to take home—suits that he was still purchasing, though he was now more than financially secure, from Goodwill, so he could invest every spare penny to make sure that in old age he was never a burden on others, and that he could leave sizable nest eggs for those he deemed most deserving.

When Dad retired and moved back to Tampa, it was a long-held dream at last realized. But his "golden years" were tarnished. He lamented to me that he never was allowed to fully enjoy them; someone followed him there whom he wished, to no avail, that he could disengage from his life. Then, the last thirteen months of Dad's life, he experienced almost unbearable levels of stress. Dad became unwittingly and inextricably immersed in a web of deceit, broken promises, and betrayal. On September 17, 2011, eleven all too brief years after fulfilling his aspiration to return to live in the beloved city of his childhood and youth, Dad was dead.

I say now, in front of his tombstone, "I'm so sorry, Dad." In the end, I wasn't there to look over him, care for him, protect him, when he was at his most fragile and vulnerable.

The last time I saw my dad asleep was when he and my family had a reunion at a Florida resort some months before he died. He was curled on the sofa late one night like a child, a pillow between his knees. While he slept deeply, I caressed his hair, his hands. Before all was said and done, he and I had bridged all differences and rediscovered the transcendent love we had for one another—a love that was always there but sometimes can get buried, or bury itself.

Now more than ever, everything I do to bring some love and joy and understanding to the world, I do for Dad—for all he was and wasn't—I do for myself—for all I am and am not—for my daughters—for all they are and will be—for my wife—for all she is, day in and day out, and will forever be. Not just for them much less for me, but beginning with them, expanding outward, forward, upward, backward from there. It makes it possible to bear and love and hope, to distill good even out of evil, and to love even the loveless and the hate filled with all my might and mind and, as much as humanly possible, without rancor or resentment.

Before leaving the gravesite, I say, my voice just above a whisper, "You've earned your sleep, Dad. Please rest in peace now." And once more: "I love you."

Part II

Soul of Goodness

THE SOUL OF A NURSE

By the time I arrive at my home airport, every single one of my events and presentations for the remainder of 2020 and the first half of 2021 around the world has been canceled or postponed indefinitely because of the unfolding pandemic. In fact, it's while I'm waiting for an Uber driver to take me from the airport to my home that I receive word that the final event of mine that was still scheduled has now also been canceled—my keynote at the international book fair in Riyadh, Saudi Arabia.

Socrates Cafés have spread throughout the Middle East these last several years, nowhere more so than Saudi Arabia and Bahrain, thanks to the enthusiastic efforts of Hadi Alshaikhnasser. A medical doctor, while doing his post-residency in the United States, Hadi regularly attended the original Socrates Café I'd started in Montclair, New Jersey, in 1996 and that still meets weekly. When he returned to Saudi Arabia, he established a number of Socrates Cafés. My book *Socrates Café* was translated into Arabic by Hadi himself after he returned, and was published in early 2020 by a prominent publishing house in Riyadh.

Of all the scheduled engagements of mine that were now canceled, this was the most disappointing and dispiriting. After the book fair, Hadi and I had planned to travel throughout Saudi Arabia, holding Socratic communions with all those taking part in the various groups he'd been instrumental in establishing. Besides Hadi, another person I had particularly looked forward to meeting in person was Ayasha, a twenty-nine-year-old nurse at a public hospital who attends a Socrates Café. During my Uber drive home, she sends me a WhatsApp message: "Just heard the news. So sad."

The mother of two had written to me to say that she found the Socrates Cafés to be among the most meaningful experiences of her life—not just for the intellectual stimulation of being with so many "deep thinkers," as she calls them, but because they helped her see the world in new lights whenever she considered the heartfelt truths that others shared and held just as passionately as she did her own. She told me she had wanted to study philosophy at university, but that at the time it wasn't permitted for women, and so she devoured philosophy books as an autodidact—and that her long-held dream was still to one day be a philosophy professor by day and a nurse by night.

Ayasha had wanted to be a nurse since a child, since her father, an engineer, had read to her about Rufaidah Al-Asalmiya. The first Muslim nurse, who lived in Saudi Arabia during the lifetime of the prophet Muhammad in the eighth century (long before Florence Nightingale), Rufaidah is a role model beloved by modern nurses in the Middle East for her indefatigable efforts to promote community health, and for establishing the first rigorous training program for nurses. Despite the low pay, high turnover, and overlong hours, Ayasha loves what she does.

I took part in one Socrates Café exchange with her and a number of other Saudi women on a WhatsApp list she'd set up. We had explored "What is the best way to show you care?" I was enrapt, during the discourse, when Ayasha shared with passion and authority Martin Heidegger's philosophy of care. She explained to us Heidegger's assertion in his masterwork *Being and Time* that *Sorge*—the desire to "attend to" and "care for" the world—is, to her, at the heart of authentic human being. To Heidegger, as Ayasha shared, *Sorge*, which literally translates as "care," represents the two fundamental human dispositions—attending to others, and being in their presence fully—that we all need to practice to make ours a heart-shaped world. "By caring for others, you also are being cared for," she told us, "and doing so with an eye towards the future. Because this is a way of caring for the well-being of the world itself." She said her calling as a nurse is her way of fulfilling this Heideggerian disposition.

At this moment, the divorced mother of two writes me a series of messages; Ayasha is on a one-hour break from her shift at the hospital. She says she and her fellow nurses don't have all the protective gear they need, making it difficult to properly care for their patients. She says that her first patient with coronavirus, a man in his sixties with underlying conditions, died, and that she is taking it hard. "About an hour before he passed, he'd asked me to pray with him," she writes to me. "And I recited the *Shahadah*, the Muslim profession of faith. We consider it a supremely caring action. And I had used the words '*Insha' Allah*'—it is Allah's will—to reassure him that he would improve. But then he died. It has shaken me."

She then tells me she is planning to take leave from her job, even if it means that she loses it. "I can't risk passing on the virus to my children. Right now, I should be there full-time for them at home, taking care of them. I won't let them go to school, even though it hasn't yet been officially closed."

Ayasha sends me a photo of herself in a hijab and burqa with her two adoring children. Just then I arrive home. My own adoring children come outside, jumping up and down, there with my loving wife, when they see me. I send Ayasha a blurry photo of our unfolding joyful reunion.

I don't have time to read her long final message until about an hour later.

> Stay safe with your beautiful family. Eventually our universe will return to its normal dimensions. This is most definitely not the end of the world! This time of isolation is a form of active life, and will give us a necessary breather so we can better decide what to do, and what not to do, for this next part of our life—a life that belongs to us alone.
>
> We must use this quarantine to discover more about our separate selves, but in a way that allows us to live more connected to others, to live without borders. It's good to have this opportunity to be alone for a while, in our little world, and to care for and love those who mean the most to us—but only if in the end it shows us how to be more caring and loving to one and all.
>
> *Khuda hafiz* (may God keep you safe).

A WALK IN THE PARK

Later that same night, my older daughter Cali, almost fourteen, and I resume our tradition of taking a walk around and around the circumference of the small park near our home. She's not fond of holding hands with me anymore, but thankfully she lets me put my arm around her. Besides more typical father-and-daughter conversations, she and I have had numerous one-on-one Socrates Cafés—most of which I post on my Socrates Café YouTube channel—beginning when she was a toddler. Questions we've explored over the years include "Can family members be friends?" "What is a good school?" "When does change do you some good, and when doesn't it?" "Does Santa exist?"

We walk in silence for a while. Then she says, "Dad, I miss Grandpa Alex."

"I do too, sweetheart."

"Why couldn't we say goodbye to him?"

"There are some damaged people in this world, my love."

"I say hello and goodbye to Grandpa every day, Dad. When I wake up and when I go to bed. I tell him about my day, about my hopes and dreams."

"I do pretty much the same thing, sweetheart. I've learned a lot during this trip about how best to honor him in all I strive to do."

"Late at night, when she can't sleep, Cybele asks me about Grandpa," Cali eventually says, referring to her six-year-old sister, named after the Greek goddess of nature and healing. "I try to tell her everything I remember about him. She cries sometimes. She's so sad that they never will get to know one another. They would have really hit it off." Indeed they would have—not just because of their shared love of devouring popcorn and eating crushed ice, but their mutual impassioned love of music, of dance, of questioning.

Not long after I arrived home from my journey, Cybele had taken me by the hand and led me to my office. "I made something for you," she said. On my coffee table, she had made an altar of her grandpa, my father. It had some of my favorite framed photos, with vases of fresh flowers, as well as several drawings she made, all of which say, "I love you Grandpa."

"I put it on the coffee table in front of your desk so you can look at your daddy and think about him and be inspired by him all the time," she said.

"It is beautiful," I told her, and I broke into tears.

I eventually asked Cybele, "Why did you put some of my books on the altar?"

"Because you said it's thanks to Grandpa, and to Grandma, that you were able to become a writer and make your dreams come true. Your books connect you and Grandpa. And so now, whenever you get writer's block on the books you're writing these days, you can just look at the altar for Grandpa for inspiration."

I think about this as Cali and I continue our walk. Then Cali says to me, "Dad, I'm afraid you're going to die. I want you to live to be over a hundred."

I think hard about how to reply. It must be so difficult to have a father who is much older in years than all her friends' fathers. "I don't know what to tell you, sweetheart. Any of us might die at any time. But I do think that, with a bit of good fortune, I'll live a long time, especially since you and Mommy and Cybele take such good care of me."

"When you can't walk anymore, I'll push you around the park in your wheelchair," she says, her eyes glowing with love.

"Cali, too many people spend too much time worrying about dying," I eventually say. "Every second we spend worrying about dying is a precious second we're not living to the fullest here and now." I think of Martin Heidegger and his truisms that everyone— everyone—has great anxiety about death and dying, and that it is the most natural thing in the world. To the contrary, all too many have great anxiety toward life and living, to giving their mortal moment everything they have.

I go on to tell Cali that I truly believe that those of us in a position to do so should live life to the utmost, never quite knowing when our time is up; and not in a morbid way, but that shows how much we care for others and for the world itself. "We each need to find a purposeful project that can contribute to that caring," I say to her.

Her brow furrowed, Cali thinks long and hard about this.

"You know what I'm going to do, Dad? I'm going to open a sanctuary to give a loving home for all the stray cats around here. I want all cats to live out their days feeling as loved and sheltered and spoiled as our own cat Twinkle."

"What a great idea, sweetheart."

"I'm going to start tomorrow, Dad. No, I'm going to draw up my plan of action for making this come true as soon as we get home."

"But it's late. Don't you want to wait till morning?"

"No," she says adamantly. "The stray cats need me too much. I can't wait a single day longer to convert this sanctuary plan of mine from dream to reality."

A DESIRE FOR GOODNESS

I'm blessed to have a family that epitomizes goodness.

Plato's *Apology*, which recounts Socrates's last moments alive and offers a rousing justification for why living and dying a certain way is its own reward, is widely considered one of the most stirring dramas ever, real life or otherwise. Far lesser known is the fact that Xenophon—who I believe was not only an excellent historian but a proficient philosopher in his own right—wrote his own eloquent set of grounds justifying Socrates's mode of being. He harnesses an array of evidence that both offers a robust defense and rebuts the charges made against Socrates that led to his death sentence:

> The indictment against him was to this effect: Socrates is guilty of rejecting the gods acknowledged by the state and of bringing in strange deities: he is also guilty of corrupting the youth. . . . [Yet] he offered sacrifices constantly, . . . now in his home, now at the altars of the state temples. . . . Moreover, Socrates lived ever in the open; . . . he passed just where most people were to be met: he was generally talking, and anyone might listen. Yet none ever knew him to offend against piety and religion in deed or word.

Just as importantly, Xenophon stresses, Socrates's "own conversation was ever of human things":

> The problems he discussed were, What is godly, what is ungod-
> ly; what is beautiful, what is ugly; what is just, what is unjust;
> what is prudence, what is madness; what is courage, what is
> cowardice; what is a state, what is a statesman; what is govern-
> ment, and what is a governor;—these and others like them.

Arriving at further and deeper answers contributes to one's understanding of the gods themselves, Xenophon asserts, since they
know all these things. Far from being a rebellious "freethinker,"
Socrates "never said or did anything contrary to sound religion, and
his utterances about the gods and his behavior towards them were
the words and actions of a man who is truly religious and deserves
to be thought so."

Hence, any charge that Socrates corrupted the youth, to Xenophon, was as specious as it gets:

> In the first place, . . . in control of his own passions and appetites
> he was the strictest of men; further, in endurance of . . . every
> kind of toil he was most resolute; . . . his needs were so schooled
> to moderation that having very little he was yet very content.
> Such was his own character: how then can he have led others
> into impiety, crime, gluttony, lust, or sloth? On the contrary, he
> cured these vices in many, by putting into them a desire for
> goodness, and by giving them confidence that self-discipline
> would make them gentlemen.

Socrates was all about inculcating "a desire for goodness." In word
and deed, Xenophon stresses in his *Memorabilia*, his mentor
"showed his companions that he was a gentleman himself, and
talked most excellently of goodness and of all things that concern
man." Even the most debauched—Xenophon specifically refers to
Alcibiades and that rascal Critias—rose to their better angels and
were prudence personified in Socrates's presence, because of his
inspiring example. "Whatever is honorable, whatever is good in
conduct is the result of training, and that this is especially true of

prudence," Xenophon writes, and no one was more a poster person for such training than Socrates himself.

To Xenophon, Socrates was all about goodness, "constantly occupied" as he was "in the consideration of right and wrong, and in doing what was right and avoiding what was wrong." What did Socrates equate with doing right and as a result studiously avoid doing the wrong? According to Xenophon, Socrates explained it this way: "They live best, I think, who strive best to become as good as possible: and the pleasantest life is theirs." He went on to say that his own life couldn't have been better or pleasanter, because the life he led was the epitome "of those who are conscious that they are growing in goodness"—*kalokagathia* in Greek. To Socrates, such nobility of mind and magnanimity largely was tantamount to "growing in knowledge of what is truly useful and beneficial and good both for mankind, and for oneself as an individual"— and *this* was tantamount to healthiness of soul.

TRAGIC HERO OF GOODNESS

My father told me that his older brother, my uncle Jimmy—a blend of Socrates, Zorba, and Willie Loman, and to me an unadulterated hero of goodness—did not come home the same person after serving his tours of duty on the front lines during World War II and then the Korean conflict. Even so, Uncle Jimmy took advantage of the GI Bill to matriculate at the University of Tampa, where he was selected to Who's Who in American Colleges. He studied literature, and excelled. He then went on to law school with great expectations. But he dropped out for reasons never fully explained to me. Uncle Jimmy instead entered a career in life insurance sales, and stayed with it until he retired nearly a half century later. My uncle felt he lived in the shadow of my highly accomplished father, try as his younger brother might to impress upon him that he was the true hero of the family for his valiant service to our country.

Uncle Jimmy rarely shared with me anything about his time as a soldier. One night, though, after I started Socrates Café and was in the throes of writing my first book about my Socratic sojourns, I visited him at his house in Tampa while my father was out of town. My uncle opened up in a way he never did before or afterward.

"I saw things, had to do things," he tells me, his voice trailing off at times. "Sometimes it was kill or be killed. If you didn't do evil yourself, evil would be done to you." The anguish on his face is palpable as he says this. This is more than a memory; he is reliving an experience from then.

Uncle Jimmy gets up from his reclining chair and pulls out two beat-up books from a bookshelf. He says he'd toted them with him in his backpack throughout his tours of duty. One is Shakespeare's *Henry V*, the other Percy Bysshe Shelley's *Prometheus Unbound*. Like his mother, Uncle Jimmy is a poet, a good one. Unlike his mother, besides his natural affinity for the great Greek works of philosophy, poetry, and art, he also has a passion for Shakespeare and the Romantics (which my *yaya* didn't mind so much after he pointed out to her how much they were influenced by the likes of Homer and Sophocles).

While tremendously pleased by my Socrates Café renown, Uncle Jimmy is, if anything, even more proud of the fact that my own poetry has been published in prominent journals, including the same issues that featured works by the likes of Charles Bukowski, who like me was a late bloomer. Bukowski wrote about desolation and abandonment; I mostly write about searching, and death.

Uncle Jimmy tells me he'd been introduced to these two particular works by his first serious love (not Greek, to his mother's dismay) of young adulthood. She'd given him the now-frayed volumes just before he left for boot camp in South Carolina. They were the entryway to what would become a lifelong love on his part of Shakespeare and of the Romantics—his specialty area of literary study when he was an undergraduate college student. *Henry V* and *Prometheus Unbound* have remained favorites of his throughout the years, the two works that spoke to him the most.

Uncle Jimmy opens *Henry V* to a severely dog-eared page and reads: "There is some soul of goodness in things evil, would men observingly distill it out." Then he looks up. "Modern war isn't like something from *The Iliad* in which degrees of right and might can be on both warring sides. Nothing glorious or romantic about our war to defeat Hitler and Mussolini, Christos. But it can have some soul of goodness if you're fighting on the right side—not the perfect side, but clearly the right side. In World War II, we had to commit the necessary evil of waging battle, of killing, to defeat an enemy that wanted to turn out the lights on humanity. In Korea, the leaders of our opponents were barbaric, committing mass slaughters. Evil things sometimes had to be done to prevent greater evil." He falls silent. "Good people died on the front lines. Both sides. Loving husbands, fathers, who had no choice but to serve, who just wanted to get home to their families. Not fair or right that I survived when many in my band of brothers didn't. Not fair or right we had to do things, no matter how necessary, you should never have to do."

We sit across from one another in comfortable silence. Much later during this sleepless night, Uncle Jimmy says to me, "When I came home from the Korean War, I was determined to have a good career, a loving family. It started out well." He shakes his head. "Started out well . . . and there were some beautiful moments over the years. I treasure the highs I was blessed to have in my personal and professional life, mourn some of the lows."

My uncle confides that, at one low point, he became estranged from his family, his career momentarily in a tailspin. He tells me that he reached such a nadir of despair that he drove his car along the causeway between Tampa and St. Petersburg, turning off the road at an isolated section of the causeway beach. He tells me, his voice at times halting, at others trailing off, that his plan was to press his foot all the way down on the accelerator and drive his car into the water, the windows rolled down, at full speed. "I sat in the car, revved the motor on and off, I don't know for how long. I had the car in park, but my hand was positioned to shift it to drive.

"I didn't go through with it." Uncle Jimmy tells me he directed his car back on the causeway and he returned home. He says he went to his office, and wrote poem after poem, until he'd worked his way through his sense of abandonment, loss, setback, and the anger that stemmed from that, until he'd confronted, through this creative act, deep-rooted grief, remorse, and guilt. He says he tore up the poems afterward; they'd served their purpose and they weren't meant for other eyes.

My uncle then opens *Prometheus Unbound*, to (if possible) an even more creased and dog-eared page. He reads in his gravelly voice, "To suffer woes which Hope thinks infinite; to forgive wrongs darker than death or night; To defy Power, which seems omnipotent; To love, and bear; to hope till Hope creates from its own wreck the thing it contemplates. Neither to change nor falter nor repent; This . . . is to be Good, great and joyous, beautiful and free."

Eventually he says, "I did suffer woes that at times I thought infinite. But at some point I decided, 'Enough.' I had to get busy living. I willed myself to hope again, and to channel that hope in ways that create from its own wreck the thing it contemplates. I took on a meaningful informal project to talk with other vets going through difficult times, and in a way it helped remake and give new meaning to my own past. When you do that, you no longer feel the need to change or falter or repent."

A long silence ensues. Uncle Jimmy seems lost in thought. Finally he says, "One order I was given as a soldier, Christos, I refused. Defied power omnipotent. I was willing to face the consequences, but it turned out I didn't have to, though I didn't know it at the time I defied it. I can't say any more about it than that. But there are some lines you cannot cross, or you wouldn't be able to forgive yourself afterwards. Some lines you cannot cross."

"But what do you do when someone does cross that line, and you are on the receiving end?" I ask him.

His looks at me: "Tell me, Christos. Tell me what happened."

At that moment, I feel an extraordinary level of trust and closeness with my uncle. I share with him something I'd never told another soul: a wrong done to me one weekend when I was not yet a teenager, when my parents were away and I was left at home. It left me traumatized, terrorized. For years afterward, I had paralyzing panic attacks. At one point, in my late twenties, I experienced a numbing depression. A darkness like death or unseeing night. I did not know how to seek professional help. I sought solace mostly in the written words of others; and in my own poetry, fiction, and nonfiction; and in music.

Uncle Jimmy's cheeks are wet. "What happened to you is a diabolical thing, Christos." He says a great deal more, and gives me a good amount of guidance, based on his own experiences with post-traumatic stress disorder.

Then he says to me, "Makes me admire even more what you've accomplished. Your dad says you're the best of us. He calls you the peacemaker in the family.

"Your dad told me once," he then says with a hint of a smile, "that when you were little you locked him and your mom inside their bedroom by tying a taut string between the doorknobs of your bedroom and theirs. You said you wouldn't let them out until they quit fighting. It got them to stop. He said he spanked you afterwards. I bet he never apologized to you." He's right. "He may have resented what you did at the moment, but deep down, he admired you for it. Your intentions were honorable, and it took a lot of courage for one so little and young. You defied power omnipotent—an explosively angry and very strong dad in your case."

As the sun peeks through the curtains, Uncle Jimmy runs his hands through his thick, graying curls and says, "Christos, people who do evil aren't that different from you and me. Something went wrong with them. Just one experience—especially in childhood—can cause them lasting damage. 'There but for the grace of God go I.' Even the worst man or woman you can think of isn't totally a devil or monster, even if they do devilish, monstrous things."

Shortly after that memorable visit, Uncle Jimmy left on his eighth trip to Nisyros. He'd said it was the only place he'd ever found peace of mind and heart. He'd journeyed there over the decades regardless of whether he could afford to. He knew my dad and I planned to go there together. "Be sure one of the first things you do is go to the acropolis and look out from the top of the wall," he told me before we parted company that night. "You'll feel things there, see things there, experience things, that people like you and me can't anyplace else."

Not long after his final visit to Nisyros, ten days before the horrors of September 11, 2001, Uncle Jimmy died. It was my father who discovered him, in the bathtub at his home, dead from a massive stroke. Uncle Jimmy left most of his few material possessions of any financial worth to his immediate loved ones. He left my father some books that to him were precious and two quite valuable rings, precious keepsakes he'd received and worn, including one for his service (like most everything in my father's home of value, the rings "disappeared" from the premises around the time of his death).

My dad was inconsolable over losing his older brother. Dad was one of the few who'd ever understood all Uncle Jimmy had suffered as a soldier, witnessing and experiencing directly man's inhumanity to man, and how it had impacted a life full of such promise. Behind his conventional exterior, and his high-level post with the Department of Defense after serving in the military himself, lurked a progressive in the sense that Dad believed the U.S. had become too imperialistic for its own good. He opposed the Vietnam War from day one of our involvement in it. Dad believed in a strong military, but he was against unnecessary wars or military interventions that were in effect power plays (he was livid over the military junta in Greece, between 1967 and 1973, more or less the same time frame as the Vietnam conflict). The last time Dad believed that U.S. military involvement was warranted was World War II.

He told me we had no business involving ourselves in Korea, much less Vietnam (he didn't buy for a second LBJ's "domino theory"). He believed our escalating participation actually set back efforts to spread democracy abroad. Most of all, Dad was aggrieved by the psychic scars that had stricken his brother because of his tours of duty in World War II and the Korean conflict. He told me how grateful he was that neither I nor my older brother faced conscription; we were fourteen and sixteen years old at the time our troops were finally pulled out. Because I never was asked to serve my country, I periodically asked myself, starting at a young age, what I could do for it; I answered my question again and again at various stages, putting my answers into action, from my UNICEF volunteer work to Socrates Café.

Uncle Jimmy is my beloved tragic hero and the epitome of goodness. Like Socrates, he had uncompromising moral courage mixed with a defiant obstinacy, demonstrated by his refusal to cross a moral line that would have made life less worth living. Uncle Jimmy did his utmost in his way to face unflinchingly demons not of his making. He was a great man who by establishment benchmarks failed in telling respects. In my book, though, and that of anyone who prizes courage, honesty, and integrity above popular notions of success, Uncle Jimmy was a tragic and accomplished hero.

Socrates himself was an abject failure in his lifetime. He failed in his effort to "rehabilitate" Alcibiades. He failed to arrest Athens' downward descent. It doesn't make his deeds less noble or heroic, but more. The odds of succeeding were impossibly against him. He did the right thing anyhow, without the slightest expectation he'd go to "a better place" after death. It didn't much matter to him what, if anything, lay next. Like my uncle Jimmy, he believed a life lived a certain way, here and now, was its own reward.

DROP OF GOODNESS

"**G**racefulness is part of the graciousness of the great-souled," writes Friedrich Nietzsche in *Twilight of the Idols*. No one to him was more a real-life ideal of such a person than Socrates. In *The Gay Science*, he extolls the indomitable Athenian as a

> genius of the heart . . . whose voice knows how to descend into the depths of every soul . . . who teaches one to listen, who smooths rough souls and lets them taste a new yearning . . . who divines the hidden and forgotten treasure, the drop of goodness . . . from whose touch everyone goes away richer, not having found grace nor amazed, not as blessed and oppressed by the good of another, but richer in himself, opened . . . less sure perhaps . . . but full of hopes that as yet have no name.

In my own lifetime of experiences "Socratizing," I have only come to differ with Nietzsche in his characterization of Socrates as someone who descended into the depths of others' souls. To the contrary, Socrates made it possible for those with whom he inquired to descend into the depths of their own souls and sculpt their own life-affirming ethic.

Out of that deep dive, those he encountered were far better able to nurture that "drop of goodness"—this is tantamount to what Plato characterized as a healthy soul.

Plato elaborates a paradigm-shattering conception of what it is to have a healthy soul in his *Republic*. For all intents and purposes, he was describing his mentor Socrates—but also that paradigmatic autonomous persona of fiction, Antigone. To Plato, such a person is ipso facto ethical, *regardless* of prevailing ethical mores. In Antigone's case, she obeyed a higher law, rejecting the ukase of King Creon in order to bury her brother Polynices, as her gods dictated. The king sentenced her to be buried alive. By the time he had a last-minute change of heart, she'd taken her death into her own hands and hanged herself rather than suffer from the king's barbaric form of execution. Likewise, Socrates was sentenced to death for his pious impiety, daring to be autonomous, out of an abiding sense of social conscience. He was found guilty of "corrupting" the youth around him by modeling for them how to think for themselves, out of a sense of mission he carried out in obeisance to a different pantheon of gods than the state-sponsored ones (also a capital crime) that gave license to the pervading sickness in his society.

No one recognized the linkage between, and drilled down into, Plato's conception of a healthy soul and Shakespeare's "soul of goodness" like the American transcendentalist philosopher Ralph Waldo Emerson. He is the only writer and thinker I've ever come across to link the two conceptions. In "Character," Emerson tells us that

> a healthy soul stands united with the Just and the True, as the magnet arranges itself with the pole; so that he stands to all beholders like a transparent object betwixt them and the sun, and whoso journeys towards the sun, journeys towards that person. He is thus the medium of the highest influence to all who are not on the same level. Thus, men of character are the conscience of the society to which they belong.

Such a soul is the epitome of autonomy and social conscience, which aren't at opposite ends of a continuum but inseparable. Emerson then goes on to say that one with a soul of goodness escapes from any set of circumstances; whilst prosperity belongs to a certain mind, and will introduce that power and victory which is its natural fruit, into any order of events.

No matter the circumstance, such a soul is Houdini-like in the sense that not even the most suffocating, oppressive set of circumstances or tragic events can contain or defeat his or her spirit. Just the opposite. The more concerted the attempt to constrict, the more malignant the effort to undermine, the more such a spirit is set free, united as it is with a soul of the just and the true. Think the fictional Antigone, the real Nelson Mandela, Sojourner Truth, Malala Yousafzai, Edith Cowan, Shirley Colleen Smith, Chiune Sugihara. Not to mention Socrates, no more so than when he cashed in his mortal chips.

Such people live by their own moral codes. They know that there is the potential for good and evil in many more than we might care to acknowledge, and that but for a circumstance here, a turn of events there, some or even many of us might have turned out far differently than we have. They knew themselves through and through, and so they felt little compunction to judge and label others in pejorative or cardboard-cutout ways; rather, they tried to heal those who had maladies of many sorts. They embody the great-souled persons extolled in Shakespeare's ninety-fourth sonnet:

> They that have power to hurt and will do none,
> That do not do the thing they most do show, . . .
> They rightly do inherit heaven's graces
> And husband nature's riches from expense;
> They are the lords and owners of their faces.

SHALL WE DANCE?

"Shall we dance?" I say to my bride Ceci, true lord and owner of her face who has rightly inherited heaven's graces, on our twenty-second wedding anniversary. Ceci and I are on our patio. Unable to go out to our favorite jazz night spot to celebrate because of the coronavirus pandemic lockdown, we have fashioned a dance space for ourselves. One of our favorite songs, "Acid" by the late, great conga drummer and band leader Ray Barreto, is wafting from our stereo.

My arms outstretched, Ceci places her hands in mine. I draw her in close. Our eyes meet, and time melts away. Dance and love is all. Among my most treasured memories of my parents is when they were in one another's company dancing. Dad was the show-off, Mom the more elegant and expert. Together, they blended seamlessly. Dance was their saving grace, in many ways the glue of their relationship. When I was a child, few things filled me with more joy than watching them dancing in one another's arms.

Dance in various forms has also been an unbroken thread throughout my years with Ceci. When I met her in 1996, she'd just journeyed from Chiapas, Mexico, to Montclair State University in northern New Jersey to earn her graduate degree in education. Though her academic studies were intensive, she somehow found time to venture to New York City each weekend to continue her training, which she'd begun in her teen years, at Martha Graham School. She also found time to take a weekly lesson with yours truly.

Ceci and I took our first dance class together in the fall of 1996, after spotting an announcement posted on the bulletin board at the café where I first convened a weekly Socrates Café. It promised to teach us western swing, salsa, rumba. Until then, my relationship with dance had been of a wayward, styleless seventies sort. I demonstrated remarkable ineptness at mastering even the most basic steps during those first classes. But my frustration was mitigated by Ceci's patient encouragement and kind insistence that she couldn't have asked for a better partner. Her movements were ethereal, languorous. I stayed with it, practiced on my own in my spare time. I got better. I learned to guide Ceci. Over time, I became less self-conscious and more skillful in tandem, and even became practiced enough to lose myself on occasion in the rhythm.

Ceci studied philosophy as an undergraduate in Mexico City. While her thesis (at her elite college, even undergraduates write theses) explored in depth the entwined ethical and educational values of contemporary Mayan women, she also was drawn to several canonical Western thinkers, first and foremost the German philosopher and social critic Friedrich Nietzsche—who was a devotee of dance. Ceci and I subscribe to Nietzsche's conception of what dance amounts to; it encompasses, as he puts it in *Twilight of the Idols*, "dancing with the feet, with ideas, with words." He might have noted that dance itself can be a searching and probing inquiry with no final destination.

Dancing at its most sublime, to Ceci, is of that sort. At age fifteen, she was among the select few who auditioned and was subsequently accepted in the Martha Graham School. Several times a week, she traversed teeming, sprawling Mexico City, braving on her own its dicey public transit system, to arrive at the dance studio.

Nothing could waylay her from immersing herself in the world of modern and jazz dance and ballet, even though she would then have to return home, traveling alone, in the late hours. While an undergraduate student, Ceci continued her commitment with dance while juggling her demanding university studies. She reluctantly parted company with the Martha Graham School for a spell when she moved to Chiapas in 1994, where she lived and worked as an educator in a Tseltal indigenous community (while there she mastered some forms of traditional Mayan dancing) before embarking in the summer of 1996 on graduate studies in the U.S., after receiving a scholarship and stipend, at a university that thankfully was in close proximity to the Martha Graham School's headquarters in Manhattan.

My relationship with Ceci started out as a dance of minds in late summer 1996, at a Socrates Café I convened in Montclair, New Jersey. Ceci, who had recently matriculated in a vaunted graduate school program that specialized in teaching philosophy for children, was the sole person who showed up at that particular philosophical soiree of mine. She and I sat across from one another at a table, and we explored the question, "What is love?," that she'd proposed. I was so taken by her beauty that I didn't always attend carefully to the philosophical pearls she shared. When I abstractedly asked her the same question more than once, she repeated her response, the picture of politeness. She knew what was what. But I do remember distinctly one thing Ceci said to me during that fateful encounter: "Love is a response. Love is something to be expressed, to be demonstrated, and it leads to this sublime place that is within us but also transcends us. But this place is very, very hard to reach." Near the midpoint of our tête-à-tête, my concentration still wavering wildly, it occurred to me that if all unfolded as the diehard romantic in me already dared it might, I'd have abundant opportunities in the future to continue exploring this eternal question with her.

We married eighteen months later. Ceci has been my modern Diotima, a reincarnation of Socrates's great teacher about love, a whirling dervish of piercing insights on matters of the mind and heart. Over the years, we have explored thousands of questions— some just between the two of us, some with the thousands of people around the globe who've engaged with us in a Socrates Café inquiry, others with our two daughters—Cali, who lives for aerial dance and rhythmic gymnastics, and who entered the world with the assistance of a midwife exactly ten years to the day Ceci and I first met, and Cybele, born in 2013, also by midwife, at Pennsylvania Hospital, the oldest hospital in the U.S., on our nation's real Independence Day, July 2, and who's never met a rhythm she didn't like and couldn't make the most of (little wonder she is now playing lead roles in musicals like *Annie*).

Anyone who has taken part in a Socrates Café experiences a kind of dance, a do-si-do in which all involved link figurative hands and hearts as they circle in and around and into a theme; they twirl around and about this idea and that, taking a deep dive that at the same time can launch one on a free flight to places heretofore unknown. Dance, too, can be an inquiry, a spirited delving into and scrutiny of dimensions for which words don't suffice; it ideally makes me a better life partner, lover, dad, human. Dance heightens my romance with life and those in it.

Nietzsche characterizes dance as "a blissful, peaceful state of motion. It is the artist's and the philosopher's vision of happiness." Now, twenty-three and a half years after we first met, my bride and I are as one as we dance to the Afro-Cuban "Acid." As many times as we've danced to this song, we never tire of it—if anything, it gets fresher with age. On each occasion, a distance is bridged, a chasm traversed, two hearts beating as one. Tenses and spaces have lost their significance.

Ceci's father passed away, at age seventy-four, six months before mine. She still grieves from her own deep loss. In almost any other country, the medical negligence and incompetence to which her father, with whom she was extremely close, was subjected would have been deemed criminal. Ceci took up Buddhistic practices after his death. It proved a most meaningful way to cope with her own suffering. Her father (for me the Platonic ideal of a father-in-law) had been a devotee of Buddhism, and her own practice of this faith and its wisdom traditions made her feel closer to him. Her smile is as effervescent as ever, but her eyes now are shot through with the pain of the loss, a pain that can never be altogether effaced.

Ceci is Percy Bysshe Shelley's ideal. She channels suffering, forgiveness, love, and forbearance in ways that make all of us in her circle, inside of which there is infinite space, better, greater, more joyous, beautiful, and free.

I never dreamed I would be loved, could be loved, like Ceci loves me. When the time arrives for me to meet my maker, if I am granted one wish, it is that no matter when or how I die, or what I die of, that I do so in her arms.

We dance the night away. Did I need to journey to many parts of the world and encounter so many thoughtful souls to learn further lessons about love and forgiveness, overcoming and understanding? After all, I have Ceci. There is also this epiphany: I understand and appreciate, more so than ever since my travels and my return home, that the kind of intoxicating, liberating, soulful conversations I had during my travels, and that I have enjoyed continually with Ceci over the years, in and of themselves make it far more possible for me to suffer, forgive, love, and bear; to be good, great, joyous, beautiful, and free.

Right at this moment, I am not so much swept up in the music and the moment as I am—as we are—the moment, two beings interlaced with graceful and gracious being. I see my face reflected in Ceci's bright eyes; it shows, like hers, a childlike exuberance, an ecstatic state that can only be had when you've emerged, with the one you love most, on the other side of despair and heartache with greater understanding and joyousness.

Until our next dance, my love, my soul of goodness.

ACKNOWLEDGMENTS

When I sent the manuscript for *Soul of Goodness* to Jonathan Kurtz, publisher of Prometheus Books, I had an inkling that this book of mine would find its ideal home here. I have long been an aficionado of Prometheus and its ancillary works. In my twenties, threadbare though my pockets were at the time, I'd subscribed to its one-of-a-kind journal *Free Inquiry*, created by Jonathan's late father, the eminent philosopher Paul Kurtz, who founded the Center for Inquiry. Like me, Dr. Kurtz was an admirer of the works of naturalist-pragmatist philosophers like Sidney Hook, about whom he'd written an exquisite book. I'm thankful to Jonathan for embracing *Soul of Goodness*, and as I told him early on (and we both agreed), I believe his father would be thrilled by our collaboration, as would my own father, Alexander (née Alexandros) Phillips.

Above and beyond my amazing and brilliant life partner Ceci—we will have been inseparable for more than twenty-five years at the time of this book's publication—without whose abiding love I would be unmoored, and Dr. Cornel West, whose unswerving support and steadfast friendship is a daily blessing, there is just no overstating the boundless loving support and belief in my works and deeds of Paul Martin, founder and CIO of Martin Capital Advisors (for whom I am an investment advisor representative); Yosef

Wosk; Dennis Karl Dienst; Karl Hebenstreit Jr.; Richard H. Bernstein, MD; Christopher C. L. McGown; and Danielle Olson. If not for these incredible souls, I would not have had the means, upon my father's passing, to find a way forward in all that I aspire to accomplish in my mortal moment.

In many respects, this is a book I would have given anything not to have had to write. But because of events swirling around my father's death, I did have to write it. I was able to see my way through in large measure also thanks to many others, notably including: Glenn Whitehouse, associate dean at Florida Gulf Coast University; Bill Sullivan, to whom I'm forever grateful for his help, of the godsend variety, way above and beyond the call of duty; Dr. Rob Carter, coauthor of *The Morning Mind*; Anas Shallal, owner of Busboys & Poets, and nonpareil civic mover and shaker; David Williams; Shep Shaw; Rob Horn; Barry, Bettylou, and Eli Kibrick; Liz Pineda; Odin Halverson; Mike Holtzclaw; Lelia Green; Kathy Cadwell; Jim Burke; Linda Pierce; the late Josie Hays; Gary and Laura Lauder; Tim Dansdill; Hadi Alshaikhnasser; Michael McCann; Sam Fairchild; John Thornell; the late Henry Outlaw; Michael Picard; Kathy Cadwell; Michael Dea; and my beloved mother, Margaret Ann P. Phillips. My gratitude and love to my family, Ceci, Cali, and Cybele are boundless; because of them, I am the most fortunate person, father, hubby. Lastly, I would like to acknowledge Dr. Arturo Romero, an orthopedic surgeon and traumatologist. Late one night on a desolate stretch of road, he literally saved me and my family from a harrowing ordeal, after hundreds of other motorists passed us by, ignoring our urgent pleas for help. When I was at my most desperate, and resigned, Dr. Romero stopped at once, intervened, and provided the needed succor. At the time, I did not know a thing about him. Not only did he refuse any recompense, he was, if anything, offended that I would think to offer it. "I did what anyone should do," he said. Thank you, Dr. Romero, a true *ningen* and soul of goodness.